Pelican Sociology
Editor: R. E. Pahl

Japanese Society

Chie Nakane is Professor of Social
Anthropology at the Institute of Oriental
Culture, University of Tokyo. She was formerly
Lecturer in Asian Anthropology at the School
of Oriental and African Studies, University of
London, and Visiting Professor in the
Department of Anthropology at the University
of Chicago. She is the author of *Kinship and
Economic Organization in Rural Japan* (1967)
and *Gharo and Khasi – A Comparative Study
in Matrilineal Systems* (1967).

D1115505

Japanese Society

Chie Nakane

Penguin Books

Penguin Books Ltd, Harmondsworth,
Middlesex, England
Penguin Books Australia Ltd, Ringwood,
Victoria, Australia

First published by Weidenfeld & Nicolson 1970
Revised edition published in Pelican Books 1973

Copyright © Chie Nakane, 1970, 1973

Made and printed in Great Britain by
Hazell Watson & Viney Ltd, Aylesbury, Bucks
Set in Linotype Times

Contents

Preface

This short work presents a configuration of the important elements to be found in contemporary Japanese social life, and attempts to shed new light on Japanese society. I deal with my own society as a social anthropologist using some of the methods which I am accustomed to applying in examining any other society. However, its form is not that of a scientific thesis (as may be seen at once from the absence of a bibliography; I have also refrained from quoting any statistical figures or precise data directly obtained from field surveys).

In this book I have tried to construct a structural image of Japanese society, synthesizing the major distinguishing features to be found in Japanese life. I have drawn evidence almost at random from a number of different types of community to be found in Japan today – industrial enterprises, government organizations, educational institutions, intellectual groups, religious communities, political parties, village communities, individual households and so on. Throughout my investigation of groups in such varied fields, I have concentrated my analysis on individual behaviour and interpersonal relations which provide the base of both the group organization and the structural tendencies dominating in the development of a group.

It may appear to some that my statements in this book are in some respects exaggerated or over-generalized; such critics might raise objections based on the observations that they themselves happen to have made. Others might object that my examples are not backed by precise or detailed data. Certainly this book does not cover the entire range of social phenomena in Japanese life, nor does it pretend to offer accurate data relevant to a particular community. This is not a description of Japanese society or culture or the Japanese people, nor an explanation of limited phenomena such as the urbanization or modernization of Japan. Rather, it is my intention that this book will offer a key (a source of intelligence and insight) to an understanding of Japanese society, and those features which are specific to it and which distinguish it from other complex societies. I have used wide-ranging suggestive evidence as material to illustrate the crucial aspects of Japanese life, for the understanding of the structural core of Japanese society rather as an artist uses his colours. I had a distinct advantage in handling these colours, for they are colours in which I was born and among which I grew up; I know their delicate shades and effects. In handling these colours, I did not employ any known sociological method and theory. Instead, I have used anything available which seemed to be effective in bringing out the core of the subject matter. This is an approach which might be closer to that of the social anthropologist than to that of the conventional sociologist.

The theoretical basis of the present work was originally established in my earlier study, *Kinship and Economic Organization in Rural Japan* (Athlone Press, London, 1967). This developed out of my own field work, including detailed monographs by others, in villages in Japan and, as soon as that research was completed, I was greatly tempted to test further, in modern society, the ideas which had emerged from my examination of a rather traditional rural society. In my view, the traditional social structure of a complex society, such as Japan, China or India, seems to persist and endure in spite of great modern changes. Hence, a further and wider exploration of my ideas, as attempted in this book, was called for in order to strengthen the theoretical basis of my earlier study.

Some of the distinguishing aspects of Japanese society which I treat in this book are not exactly new to Japanese and western observers and may be familiar from discussions in previous writings on Japan. However, my *interpretations* are different and the way in which I *synthesize* these aspects is new. Most of the sociological studies of contemporary Japan have been concerned primarily with its changing aspects, pointing to the 'traditional' and 'modern' elements as representing different or opposing qualities. The hey-day of this kind of approach came during the American occupation and in the immediately subsequent years, when it was the standpoint adopted by both Japanese and American social scientists. The tendency towards such an approach is still prevalent; it is their thesis that any phenomena which seem peculiar to Japan, not having been found in western society, can be labelled as 'feudal' or 'pre-modern' elements, and are to be regarded as contradictory or obstructive to modernization. Underneath such views, it seems that there lurks a kind of correlative and syllogistic view of social evolution: when it is completely modernized Japanese society will or should become the same as that of the west. The proponents of such views are interested either in uprooting feudal elements or in discovering and noting modern elements which are comparable to those of the west. The fabric of Japanese society has thus been made to appear to be torn into pieces of two kinds. But in fact it remains as one well-integrated entity. In my view, the 'traditional' is one aspect (not element) of the same social body which also has 'modern' features. I am more interested in the truly basic components and their potentiality in the society – in other words, in social persistence.

The persistence of social structure can be seen clearly in the modes of personal social relation which determine the probable variability of group organization in changing circumstances. This persistence reveals the basic value orientation inherent in society, and is the driving force of the development of society. Social tenacity is dependent largely on the degree of integration and the time span of the history of a society. In Japan, India, China and elsewhere, rich and well-integrated economic and social development occurred during the pre-modern period, comparable to the 'post-feudal' era in European history, and helped create a unique institutionalization of social ideals. Values that crystallized into definite form during the course of pre-modern history are deeply rooted and aid or hinder, as

Preface

the case may be, the process of modernization. To explore these values in terms of their effects on social structure appears to me to be a fascinating subject for the social sciences. In this light, I think Japan presents a rich field for the development of a theory of social structure.

I approach this issue through a structural analysis, not a cultural or historical explanation. The working of what I call the *vertical principle* in Japanese society is the theme of this book. In my view, the most characteristic feature of Japanese social organization arises from the single bond in social relationships: an individual or a group has always one single distinctive relation to the other. The working of this kind of relationship meets the unique structure of Japanese society as a whole, which contrasts to that of caste or class societies. Thus Japanese values are manifested. Some of my Japanese readers might feel repelled in the face of some parts of my discussion; where I expose certain Japanese weaknesses they might even feel considerable distaste. I do this, however, not because of a hypercritical view of the Japanese or Japanese life but because I intend to be as objective as possible in this analysis of the society to which I belong. I myself take these weaknesses for granted as elements which constitute part of the entire body which also has its great strengths.

Finally, I wish to express my profound thanks to Professor Ernest Gellner, whose very stimulating and detailed comments as editor helped me a great deal in completing the final version of the manuscript. I am greatly indebted to Professor Geoffrey Bownas, who kindly undertook the difficult task of correcting my English. I was fascinated by the way he found it possible to make my manuscript so much more readable without altering even a minor point in the flow of my discussion.

C.N.

1   Criteria of Group Formation

1. Attribute and frame

The following analysis employs two basic but contrasting criteria. These are *attribute* and *frame*, concepts newly formulated here, but which, I think, are illuminating and useful in a comparative study of Japanese and other societies.

It is important, however, to redefine our terms. In this analysis groups may be identified by applying the two criteria: one is based on the individual's common *attribute*, the other on situational position in a given *frame*. I use *frame* as a technical term with a particular significance as opposed to the criterion of *attribute*, which, again, is used specifically and in a broader sense than it normally carries. *Frame* may be a locality, an institution or a particular relationship which binds a set of individuals into one group: in all cases it indicates a criterion which sets a boundary and gives a common basis to a set of individuals who are located or involved in it. In fact, my term *frame* is the English translation of the Japanese *ba*, the concept from which I originally evolved my theory, but for which it is hard to find the exact English counterpart. *Ba* means 'location', but the normal usage of the term connotes a special base on which something is placed according to a given purpose. The term *ba* is also used in physics for 'field' in English.

Let me indicate how these two technical terms can be applied to various actual contexts. Attribute may mean, for instance, being a member of a definite descent group or caste. In contrast, being a member of X village expresses the commonality of frame. Attribute may be acquired not only by birth but by achievement. Frame is more circumstantial. These criteria serve to identify the individuals in a certain group, which can then in its turn be classified within the whole society, even though the group may or may not have a particular function of its own as a collective body. Classifications such as landlord and tenant are based on attribute, while such a unit as a landlord and his tenants is a group formed by situational position. Taking industry as an example, 'lathe operator' or 'executive' refers to attribute, but 'members of Y Company' refers to frame. In the same way, 'professor', 'office clerk' and 'student' are attributes, whereas 'men of Z University' is a frame.

In any society, individuals are gathered into social groups or social strata on the bases of attributes and frame. There may be some cases where the two factors coincide in the formation of a group, but usually they overlap each other, with individuals belonging to different groups at the same time. The primary concern in this discussion is the relative degree of function of each criterion. There are some cases where either the attribute or the frame factor functions alone, and some where the two are mutually competitive. The way in which the factors are commonly weighted bears a close reciprocal relationship to the values which develop in the social consciousness of the people in the society. For example, the group consciousness of the Japanese depends considerably on this immediate social context, frame, whereas in India it lies in attribute (most symbolically expressed in caste, which is fundamentally a social group based on the ideology of occupation and kinship). On this point, perhaps, the societies of Japan and India show the sharpest contrast, as will be discussed later in greater detail.

The ready tendency of the Japanese to stress situational position in a particular frame, rather than universal attribute, can be seen in the following example: when a Japanese 'faces the outside' (confronts another person) and affixes some position to himself socially he is inclined to give precedence to institution over kind of occupation. Rather than saying, 'I am a typesetter' or 'I am a filing clerk', he is likely to say, 'I am from B Publishing Group' or 'I belong to S Company'. Much depends on context, of course, but where a choice exists, he will use this latter form. (I will discuss later the more significant implications for Japanese social life indicated by this preference.) The listener would rather hear first about the connection with B Publishing Group or S Company; that he is a journalist or printer, engineer or office worker is of secondary importance. When a man says he is from X Television one may imagine him to be a producer or cameraman, though he may in fact be a chauffeur. (The universal business suit makes it hard to judge by appearances.) In group identification, a frame such as a 'company' or 'association' is of primary importance; the attribute of the individual is a secondary matter. The same tendency is to be found among intellectuals: among university graduates, what matters most, and functions the strongest socially, is not whether a man holds or does not hold a PhD but rather from which university he graduated. Thus the criterion by which Japanese classify individuals socially tends to be that of particular institution, rather than of universal attribute. Such group consciousness and orientation fosters the strength of an institution, and the institutional unit (such as school or company) is in fact the basis of Japanese social organization, as will be discussed extensively in Chapter Three.

The manner in which this group consciousness works is also revealed in the way the Japanese uses the expression *uchi* (my house) to mean the place of work, organization, office or school to which he belongs; and *otaku* (your house) to mean a second person's place of work and so on. The term *kaisha* symbolizes the expression of group consciousness. *Kaisha* does not mean that individuals are bound by contractual relationships into a corporate enterprise, while still thinking of themselves as separate entities; rather, *kaisha* is 'my' or 'our' company, the community to which one belongs primarily, and which is all-important in one's life. Thus in most cases the company provides the whole social existence of a person, and has authority over all aspects of his life; he is deeply emotionally involved in the association.* That Company A belongs not to its share-

---

*I find it difficult to choose an English equivalent for *kaisha*: though 'company' or 'enterprise' correspond etymologically, they do not have the social implications that the word *kaisha* has for a Japanese.

holders, but rather belongs to 'us', is the sort of reasoning involved here, which is carried to such a point that even the modern legal process must compromise in face of this strong native orientation. I would not wish to deny that in other societies an employee may have a kind of emotional attachment to the company or his employer; what distinguishes this relation in Japan is the exceedingly high degree of this emotional involvement. It is openly and frequently expressed in speech and behaviour in public as well as in private, and such expressions always receive social and moral appreciation and approbation.

The essence of this firmly rooted, latent group consciousness in Japanese society is expressed in the traditional and ubiquitous concept of *ie*, the household, a concept which penetrates every nook and cranny of Japanese society. The Japanese usage *uchi-no* referring to one's work place indeed derives from the basic concept of *ie*. The term *ie* also has implications beyond those to be found in the English words 'household' or 'family'.

The concept of *ie*, in the guise of the term 'family system', has been the subject of lengthy dispute and discussion by Japanese legal scholars and sociologists. The general consensus is that, as a consequence of modernization, particularly because of the new post-war civil code, the *ie* institution is dying. In this ideological approach the *ie* is regarded as being linked particularly with feudal moral precepts; its use as a fundamental unit of social structure has not been fully explored.

In my view, the most basic element of the *ie* institution is not that form whereby the eldest son and his wife live together with the old parents, nor an authority-structure in which the household head holds the power and so on. Rather, the *ie* is a corporate residential group and, in the case of agriculture or other similar enterprises, *ie* is a managing body. The *ie* comprises household members (in most cases the family members of the household head, but others in addition to family members may be included), who thus make up the units of a distinguishable social group. In other words, the *ie* is a social group constructed on the basis of an established frame of residence and often of management organization. What is important here is that the human relationships within this household group are thought of as more important than all other human relationships. Thus the wife and daughter-in-law who have come from outside have incomparably greater importance than one's own sisters and daughters, who have married and gone into other households. A brother, when he has built a separate house, is thought of as belonging to another unit or household; on the other hand, the son-in-law, who was once a complete outsider, takes the position of a household member and becomes more important than the brother living in another household. This is remarkably different from societies such as that of India, where the weighty factor of sibling relationship (a relationship based on commonality of attribute, that of being born of the same parents) continues paramount until death, regardless of residential circumstances; theoretically, the stronger the factor of sibling relationship, the weaker the social independence of a household as a residence unit. (It goes without saying, of course, that customs such as the adopted son-in-law system prevalent in Japan are non-existent in Hindu society. The same is true of Europe.) These facts support the theory that group-forming criteria based on functioning by attribute oppose group-forming criteria based on functioning by frame.

Naturally, the function of forming groups on the basis of the element of the frame, as demonstrated in the formation of the household, involves the possibility of including members with a differing attribute, and at the same time expelling a member who has the same attribute. This is a regular occurrence, particularly among traditional agricultural and merchant households. Not only may outsiders with not the remotest kinship tie be invited to be heirs and successors but servants and clerks are usually incorporated as members of the household and treated as family members by the head of the household. This inclusion must be accepted without reservation to ensure that when a clerk is married to the daughter of the household and becomes an adopted son-in-law the household succession will continue without disruption.

Such a principle contributes to the weakening of kinship ties.

Kinship, the core of which lies in the sibling relation, is a criterion based on attribute. Japan gives less weight to kinship than do other societies, even England; in fact, the function of kinship is comparatively weak outside the household. The saying 'the sibling is the beginning of the stranger' accurately reflects Japanese ideas on kinship. A married sibling who lives in another household is considered a kind of outsider. Towards such kin, duties and obligations are limited to the level of the seasonal exchange of greetings and presents, attendance at wedding and funeral ceremonies and the minimum help in case of accident or poverty. There are often instances where siblings differ widely in social and economic status; the elder brother may be the mayor, while his younger brother is a postman in the same city; or a brother might be a lawyer or businessman, while his widowed sister works as a domestic servant in another household. The wealthy brother normally does not help the poor brother or sister, who has set up a separate household, as long as the latter can somehow support his or her existence; by the same token, the latter will not dare to ask for help until the last grain of rice has gone. Society takes this for granted, for it gives prime importance to the individual household rather than to the kin group as a whole.

This is indeed radically different from the attitudes to kin found in India and other south east Asian countries, where individual wealth tends to be distributed among relatives; here the kin group as a whole takes precedence over the individual household and nepotism plays an important role. I have been surprised to discover that even in England and America, brothers and sisters meet much more frequently than is required by Japanese standards, and that there exists such a high degree of attachment to kinfolk. Christmas is one of the great occasions when these kinfolk gather together; New Year's Day is Japan's equivalent to the western Christmas, everyone busy with preparations for visits from subordinate staff, and then, in turn, calling on superiors. There is little time and scope to spare for collateral kin – married brothers, sisters, cousins, uncles and aunts and so on – though parents and grandparents will certainly be visited if they do not live in the same house. Even in rural areas, people say 'One's neighbour is of more importance than one's relatives' or 'You can carry on your life without cousins, but not without your neighbours'.

The kinship which is normally regarded as the primary and basic human attachment seems to be compensated in Japan by a personalized relation to a corporate group based on work, in which the major aspects of social and economic life are involved. Here again we meet the vitally important unit in Japanese society of the corporate group based on frame. In my view, this is the basic principle on which Japanese society is built.

To sum up, the principles of Japanese social group structure can be seen clearly portrayed in the household structure. The concept of this traditional household institution, *ie*, still persists in the various group identities which are termed *uchi*, a colloquial form of *ie*. These facts demonstrate that the formation of social groups on the basis of fixed frames remains characteristic of Japanese social structure.

Among groups larger than the household, there is that described by the medieval concept, *ichizoku-rōtō* (one family group and its retainers). The idea of group structure as revealed in this expression is an excellent example of the frame-based social group. This is indeed the concept of one household, in which family members and retainers are not separated but form an integrated corporate group. There are often marriage ties between the two sides of this corporate group, and all lines of distinction between them become blurred. The relationship is the same as that between family members and clerks or servants in a household. This is a theoretical antithesis to a group formed exclusively on lineage or kin.

The equivalent in modern society of *ie* and *ichizoku-rōtō* is a group such as 'One Railway Family' (*kokutetsu-ikka*), which signifies the Japanese National Railways. A union, incorporating both workers and management, calls this 'management-labour harmony'. Though it is often said that the traditional family (*ie*) institution has disappeared, the concept of the *ie* still persists in modern contexts. A company is conceived as an *ie*, all its employees qualifying as members of the household, with the employer at its head. Again this 'family' envelops the employee's personal family; it 'engages' him 'totally' (*marugakae* in Japanese). The employer readily takes responsibility for his employee's family, for which, in turn, the primary concern is the company, rather than relatives who reside elsewhere. (The features relating the company with its employees' families will be discussed later, pp. 14–15.) In this modern context, the employee's family, which normally comprises the employee himself, his wife and children, is a unit which can no longer be conceived as an *ie*, but simply a family. The unit is comparable to the family of a servant or clerk who worked in the master's *ie*, the managing body of the pre-modern enterprise. The role of the *ie* institution as the distinct unit in society in pre-modern times is now played by the company. This social group consciousness symbolized in the concept of the *ie*, of being one unit within a frame, has been achievable at any time, has been promoted by slogans and justified in the traditional morality.

This analysis calls for a reconsideration of the stereotyped view that modernization or urbanization weakens kinship ties, and creates a new type of social organization on entirely different bases. Certainly industrialization produces a new type of organization, the formal structure of which may be closely akin to that found in modern western societies. However, this does not necessarily accord with changes in the informal structure, in which, as in the case of Japan, the traditional structure persists in large measure. This demonstrates that the basic social structure continues in spite of great changes in social organization.[*]

[*] I think that, in this analysis, it is effective and convenient to employ the differentiated concepts, *social structure* and *social organization*, as proposed by Raymond Firth ('Social Organization and Social Change', *Journal of the Royal Anthropological Institute*, vol. 84, pp. 1–20, 1954; the same paper appears as Chapter III of *Essays on Social Organization and Values*, 1964).

2. Emotional participation and one-to-one relationships

It is clear from the previous section that social groups constructed with particular reference to situation, i.e. frame, include members with differing attributes. A group formed on the basis of commonality of attribute can possess a strong sense of exclusiveness, based on this homogeneity, even without recourse to any form of law. Naturally, the relative strength of this factor depends on a variety of conditional circumstances, but in the fundamentals of group formation this homogeneity among group members stands largely by its own strength, and conditions are secondary. When a group develops on the situational basis of frame the primary form is a simple herd which in itself does not possess internal positive elements which can constitute a social group. Constituent elements of the group in terms of their attributes may be heterogenous but may not be complementary. (The discussion here does not link with Durkheimian Theory as such; the distinction is between societies where people stick together because they are similar and those where they stick together because they are complementary.) For example, a group of houses built in the same area may form a village simply by virtue of physical demarcation from other houses. But in order to create a functional corporate group, there is need of an internal organization which will link these independent households. In such a situation some sort of law must be evolved to guide group coherence.

In addition to the initial requirement of a strong, enduring frame, there is need to strengthen the frame even further and to make the group element tougher. Theoretically, this can be done in two ways. One is to influence the members within the frame in such a way that they have a feeling of 'one-ness'; the second method is to create an internal organization which will tie the individuals in the group to each other and then to strengthen this organization. In practice, both these modes occur together, are bound together and progress together; they become, in fact, one common rule of action, but for the sake

9

of convenience I shall discuss them separately. In this section I discuss the feeling of unity; in the following chapter I shall consider internal organization.

People with different attributes can be led to feel that they are members of the same group, and that this feeling is justified, by stressing the group consciousness of 'us' against 'them', i.e. the external, and by fostering a feeling of rivalry against other similar groups. In this way there develops internally the sentimental tie of 'members of the same troop'.

Since disparity of attribute is a rational thing, an emotional approach is used to overcome it. This emotional approach is facilitated by continual human contact of the kind that can often intrude on those human relations which belong to the completely private and personal sphere. Consequently, the power and influence of the group not only affects and enters into the individual's actions; it alters even his ideas and ways of thinking. Individual autonomy is minimized. When this happens, the point where group or public life ends and where private life begins no longer can be distinguished. There are those who perceive this as a danger, an encroachment on their dignity as individuals; on the other hand, others feel safer in total group-consciousness. There seems little doubt that the latter group is in the majority. Their sphere of living is usually concentrated solely within the village community or the place of work. The Japanese regularly talk about their homes and love affairs with co-workers; marriage within the village community or place of work is prevalent; the family frequently participates in company pleasure trips. The provision of company housing, a regular practice among Japan's leading enterprises, is a good case in point. Such company houses are usually concentrated in a single area and form a distinct entity within, say, a suburb of a large city. In such circumstances employees' wives come into close contact with and are well informed about their husbands' activities. Thus, even in terms of physical arrangements, a company with its employees and their families forms a distinct social group. In an extreme case, a company may have a common grave for its employees, similar to the household grave. With group-consciousness so highly developed there is almost no social life outside the particular group on which an individual's major economic life depends. The individual's every problem must be solved within this frame. Thus group participation is simple and unitary. It follows then that each group or institution developes a high degree of independence and closeness, with its own internal law which is totally binding on members.

The archetype of this kind of group is the Japanese 'household' (*ie*) as we have described it in the previous section. In Japan, for example, the mother-in-law and daughter-in-law problem is preferably solved inside the household, and the luckless bride has to struggle through in isolation, without help from her own family, relatives or neighbours. By comparison, in agricultural villages in India not only can the bride make long visits to her parental home but her brother may frequently visit her and help out in various ways. Mother-in-law and daughter-in-law quarrels are conducted in raised voices that can be heard all over the neighbourhood, and when such shouting is heard all the women (of the same caste) in the neighbourhood come over to help out. The mutual assistance among the wives who come from other villages is a quite enviable factor completely unimaginable among Japanese women. Here again the function of the social factor of attribute (wife) is demonstrated; it supersedes the function of the frame of the household. In Japan, by contrast, 'the parents step in when their children quarrel' and, as I shall explain in detail later, the structure is the complete opposite to that in India.

Moral ideas such as 'the husband leads and the wife obeys' or 'man and wife are one flesh' embody the Japanese emphasis on integration. Among Indians, however, I have often observed husband and wife expressing quite contradictory opinions without the slightest hesitation. This is indeed rare in front of others in Japan. The traditional authority of the Japanese household head, once regarded as the prime characteristic of the family system, extended over the conduct, ideas and ways of thought of the household's members, and on this score the household head could be said to wield a far greater power than his Indian counterpart. In Indian family life there are all kinds of rules that apply in accordance with the status of the individual family member: the wife, for instance, must not speak directly to her husband's elder brothers, father, etc. These rules all relate to individual behaviour, but in the sphere of ideas and ways of thought the freedom and strong individuality permitted even among members of the same family is surprising to a Japanese. The rules, moreover, do not differ from household to household, but are common to the whole community, and especially among the members of the same caste community. In other words, the rules are of universal character, rather than being situational or particular to each household, as is the case in Japan.* Compared with traditional Japanese family life, the extent to which members of an Indian household are bound by the individual household's traditional practices is very small.

An Indian who had been studying in Japan for many years once compared Japanese and Indian practice in the following terms:

Why does a Japanese have to consult his companions over even the most trivial matter? The Japanese always call a conference about the slightest thing, and hold frequent meetings, though these are mostly informal, to decide everything. In India, we have definite rules as family members (and this is also true of other social groups), so that when one wants to do something one knows whether it is all right by instantaneous reflection on those rules – it is not necessary to consult with the head or with other members of the family. Outside these rules, you are largely free to act as an individual; whatever you do, you have only to ask whether or not it will run counter to the rules.

As this clearly shows, in India 'rules' are regarded as a defi-

---

*Certainly there exists what may be called a standard norm or commonality which is shared by Japanese households as a whole (or, more precisely, by a local community or different strata), but within this context each individual household normally has its own ways to regulate the behaviour and speech of individual members.

nite but abstract social form, not as a concrete and individualized form particular to each family/social group as is the case in Japan. The individuality of the Indian family unit is not strong, nor is there group participation by family members of the order of the emotional participation in the Japanese household; nor is the family as a living unit (or as a group holding communal property) a closed community as in the case of the Japanese household. Again, in contrast to Japanese practice, the individual in India is strongly tied to the social network outside his household.

In contrast to the Japanese system, the Indian system allows freedom in respect of ideas and ways of thought as opposed to conduct. I believe for this reason, even though there are economic and ethical restrictions on the modernization of society, the Indian does not see his traditional family system as an enemy of progress to such a degree as the Japanese does. This view may contradict that conventionally held by many people on the Indian family. It is important to note that the comparison here is made between Japanese and Hindu systems focused on actual interpersonal relationships within the family or household, rather than between western and Indian family patterns in a general outlook. I do not intend here to present the structure and workings of actual personal relations in Japanese and Hindu families in detail, but the following point would be of some help in indicating my thesis. In the ideal traditional household in Japan, for example, opinions of the members of the household should always be held unanimously regardless of the issue, and this normally meant that all members accepted the opinion of the household head, without even discussing the issue. An expression of a contradictory opinion to that of the head was considered a sign of misbehaviour, disturbing the harmony of the group order. Contrasted to such a unilateral process of decision making in the Japanese household, the Indian counterpart allows much room for discussion between its members; they, whether sons, wife or even daughters, are able to express their views much more freely and they in fact can enjoy a discussion, although the final decision

13

may be taken by the head. Hindu family structure is similar hierarchically to the Japanese family, but the individual's rights are well preserved in it. In the Japanese system all members of the household are in one group under the head, with no specific rights according to the status of individuals within the family. The Japanese family system differs from that of the Chinese system, where family ethics are always based on relationships between particular individuals such as father and son, brothers and sisters, parent and child, husband and wife, while in Japan they are always based on the collective group, i.e. members of a household, not on the relationships between individuals.

The Japanese system naturally produces much more frustration in the members of lower status in the hierarchy; and allows the head to abuse the group or an individual member. In Japan, especially immediately after the second world war, the idea has gained ground that the family system (*ie*) was an evil, feudalistic growth obstructing modernization, and on this premise one could point out the evil uses to which the unlimited infiltration of the household head's authority were put. It should be noticed here, however, that although the power of each individual household head is often regarded as exclusively his own, in fact it is the social group, the 'household', which has the ultimate integrating power, a power which restricts each member's behaviour and thought, including that of the household head himself.

Another group characteristic portrayed in the Japanese household can be seen when a business enterprise is viewed as a social group. In this instance a closed social group has been organized on the basis of the 'life-time employment system' and the work made central to the employees' lives. The new employee is in just about the same position and is, in fact, received by the company in much the same spirit as if he were a newly born family member, a newly adopted son-in-law or a bride come into the husband's household. A number of well-known features peculiar to the Japanese employment system illustrate this characteristic, for example, company housing,

14

hospital benefits, family recreation groups for employees, monetary gifts from the company on the occasion of marriage, birth or death and even advice from the company's consultant on family planning. What is interesting here is that this tendency is very obvious even in the most forward-looking, large enterprises or in supposedly modern, advanced management. The concept is even more evident in Japan's basic payment system, used by every industrial enterprise and government organization, in which the family allowance is the essential element. This is also echoed in the principle of the seniority payment system.

The relationship between employer and employee is not to be explained in contractual terms. The attitude of the employer is expressed by the spirit of the common saying, 'the enterprise is the people'. This affirms the belief that employer and employee are bound as one by fate in conditions which produce a tie between man and man often as firm and close as that between husband and wife. Such a relationship is manifestly not a purely contractual one between employer and employee; the employee is already a member of his own family, and all members of his family are naturally included in the larger company 'family'. Employers do not employ only a man's labour itself but really employ the total man, as is shown in the expression *marugakae* (completely enveloped). This trend can be traced consistently in Japanese management from the Meiji period to the present.

The life-time employment system, characterized by the integral and lasting commitment between employee and employer, contrasts sharply with the high mobility of the worker in the United States. It has been suggested that this system develops from Japan's economic situation and is closely related to the surplus of labour. However, as J. C. Abegglen has suggested in his penetrating analysis,* the immobility of Japanese labour is not merely an economic problem. That it is also closely related to the nature of Japanese social structure will become evident from my discussion. In fact, Japanese labour relations

*J. C. Abegglen, *The Japanese Factory*, 1958, Chapter 2.

in terms of surplus and shortage of labour have least affected the life-time employment system. Indeed, these contradictory situations have together contributed to the development of the system.

It might be appropriate at this point to give a brief description of the history of the development of the life-time employment system in Japan. In the early days of Japan's industrialization, there was a fairly high rate of movement of factory workers from company to company, just as some specific type of workmen or artisans of pre-industrial urban Japan had moved freely from job to job. Such mobility in some workers in pre-industrial and early industrial Japan seems to be attributed to the following reasons: a specific type of an occupation, the members of which consisted of a rather small percentage of the total working population and the demand for them was considerably high; these workers were located in a situation outside well established institutionalized systems. The mobility of factory workers caused uncertainty and inconvenience to employers in their efforts to retain a constant labour force. To counteract this fluidity, management policy gradually moved in the direction of keeping workers in the company for their entire working lives, rather than towards developing a system based on contractual arrangements. By the beginning of this century larger enterprises were already starting to develop management policies based on this principle; they took the form of various welfare benefits, company houses at nominal rent, commissary purchasing facilities and the like. This trend became particularly marked after the first world war when the shortage of labour was acute.

It was also at the end of the first world war that there came into practice among large companies the regular employment system by which a company takes on each spring a considerable number of boys who have just left school. This development arose from the demand for company-trained personnel adapted to the mechanized production systems that followed the introduction of new types of machinery from Germany and the United States. Boys fresh from school were the best potential labour force for mechanized industry because they were more easily moulded to suit a company's requirements. They were trained by the company not only technically but also morally. In Japan it has always been believed that individual moral and mental attitudes have an important bearing on productive power. Loyalty towards the company has been highly regarded. A man may be an excellent technician, but if his way of thought and his moral attitudes do not accord with the company's ideal the company does not hesitate to dismiss him. Men who move in from another company at a comparatively advanced stage in their working life tend to be considered difficult to mould or suspect in their loyalties. Ease of training, then, was the major reason why recruitment of workers was directed more and more towards boys fresh from school.*

Recruitment methods thus paved the way for the development of the life-employment system. An additional device was evolved to hold workers to a company, for example, the seniority payment system based on duration of service, age and educational qualifications, with the added lure of a handsome payment on retirement. The principle behind this seniority system had the advantage of being closely akin to the traditional pattern of commercial and agricultural mangement in pre-industrial Japan. In these old-style enterprises operational size had been relatively small – one household or a group of affiliated households centred on one particular household, the head of which acted as employer while his family members and affiliated members or servants acted as permanent employees. Thus the pattern of employment in a modern industrial enterprise has close structural and ideological links with traditional household management.

The shift towards life-employment was assisted in the second and third decades of this century by developments in the bureaucratic structure of business enterprises: a proliferation of sections was accompanied by finer gradings in official rank. During

*For an excellent statement of conditions, see Abegglen, op. cit., Chapter 1.

these twenty years there appeared uniforms for workers, badges (lapel buttons) worn as company insignia and stripes on the uniform cap to indicate section and rank. Workers thus came under a more rigid institutional hierarchy, but they were also given greater incentives by the expectation of climbing the delicately subdivided ladder of rank.

During the war this system was strengthened further by the adoption of a military pattern. Labour immobility was reinforced by government policy, which cut short the trend to increased mobility that had been the result of the acute shortage of labour. The prohibition on movement of labour between factories was bolstered by the moral argument that it was through concentrated service to his own factory that a worker could best serve the nation. The factory was to be considered as a household or family, in which the employer would and should care for both the material and mental life of his worker and the latter's family. According to the 'Draft of Labour Regulations' (Munitions Public Welfare Ministry Publication, February 1945):

The factory, by its production, becomes the arena for putting into practice the true aims of Imperial labour. The people who preserve these aims become the unifiers of labour. Superior and inferior should help each other, those who are of the same rank should co-operate and, with a fellowship as of one family, we shall combine labour and management.

Thus the factory's household-like function came about, in part, at the behest of state authority. In this context, a moral and patriotic attitude was regarded as more important than technical proficiency. Against shortages in the commodity market, the factory undertook to supply rice, vegetables, clothing, lodging accommodation, medical care, etc.

Familialism, welfare services and extra payments supplied by the company were thus fully developed under the peculiar circumstances of war, and have been retained as the institutional pattern in the post-war years. It is also to be noted that the process was further encouraged by post-war union activity. Unions mushroomed after the war, when 48,000 unions enrolled 9,000,000 members. These unions were formed primarily within a single company and encompassed members of different types of occupation and qualification, both staff and line workers. It is said that, in some aspects, a union is like the wartime Industrial Patriotism Club (*Sangyō-hōkoku-kai*), lacking only the company president. Thus it can serve as part of the basis of familialism. The establishment of welfare facilities, company housing schemes, recreation centres at seaside or hill resorts, etc., are all items demanded by the unions along with wage increases. Above all, the single most important union success was the gaining of the right of appeal against summary dismissal or lay-off. In the period immediately after the war dismissal meant starvation; this, together with the swiftly increasing power of the union movement, accounts for the unions' success in acquiring this tremendous privilege. Thus life employment, a policy initiated by management, has reached its perfected form through the effect of post-war unionism. Again, to combat the shortage of younger workers and highly trained engineers which is felt so acutely today, management policy is moving further towards attempts at retaining labour by the offer of more beneficial provisions.

As it has shown in the course of its development, life-time employment has advantages for both employer and employee. For the employer it serves to retain the services of skilled workers against times of labour shortage. For the employee it gives security against surplus labour conditions; whatever the market circumstances, there is little likelihood of the employee finding better employment if he once leaves his job. This system has, in fact, been encouraged by contradictory situations – shortage and surplus of labour. Here is demonstrated a radical divergence between Japan and America in management employment policy; a Japanese employer buys future potential labour and an American employer buys labour immediately required. According to the Japanese reasoning, any deficiencies in the current labour force will be compensated by the development of maximum power in the labour force of the future; the employer buys his labour material and shapes it until it best fits his production need. In America management buys ready-made labour.

Familialism, another offspring of the operational mechanism of modern industrial enterprise, is the twin to life employment. Attention has already been drawn (see p. 7) to the concept of 'The One Railway Family' which was advocated as early as 1909 by then then President of the National Railways, Gotō Shinpei. The concept was strengthened during the war years, and it has appeared in such favourite slogans of post-war management as 'the spirit of love for the company' and 'the new familialism'. According to so-called modern and advanced management theory, a genuinely inspired 'spirit of love for the company' is not merely advocated, but is indeed an atmosphere resulting from management policy, so that 'whether the feeling of love for the company thrives or not is the barometer of the abilities and talents of management staff'. Even in the coining of expressions which may seem antithetical – 'we must love our company' and 'the spirit of love for the company is silly' – the underlying motivation remains the securing of the employee's total emotional participation.

In summary, the characteristics of Japanese enterprise as a social group are, first, that the group is itself family-like and, second, that it pervades even the private lives of its employees, for each family joins extensively in the enterprise. These characteristics have been cautiously encouraged by managers and administrators consistently from the Meiji period. And the truth is that this encouragement has always succeeded and reaped rewards.

A cohesive sense of group unity, as demonstrated in the operational mechanism of household and enterprise, is essential as the foundation of the individual's total emotional participation in the group; it helps to build a closed world and results in strong group independence or isolation. This inevitably breeds household customs and company traditions. These in turn are emphasized in mottoes which bolster the sense of unity and group solidarity, and strengthen the group even more. At the same time, the independence of the group and the stability of the frame, both cultivated by this sense of unity, create a gulf between the group and others with similar attributes but outside the frame; meanwhile, the distance between people with differing attributes within the frame is narrowed and the functioning of any group formed on the base of similar attributes is paralysed. Employees in an enterprise must remain in the group, whether they like it or not: not only do they not want to change to another company; even if they desire a change, they lack the means to accomplish it. Because there is no tie between workers of the same kind, as in a 'horizontal' craft union, they get neither information nor assistance from their counterparts. (This situation is identical with that of the Japanese married-in bride as described above.) Thus, in this type of social organization, as society grows more stable, the consciousness of similar qualities becomes weaker and, conversely, the consciousness of the difference between 'our people' and 'outsiders' is sharpened.

The consciousness of 'them' and 'us' is strengthened and aggravated to the point that extreme contrasts in human relations can develop in the same society, and anyone outside 'our' people ceases to be considered human. Ridiculous situations occur, such as that of the man who will shove a stranger out of the way to take an empty seat, but will then, no matter how tired he is, give up the seat to someone he knows, particularly if that someone is a superior in his company.

An extreme example of this attitude in group behaviour is the Japanese people's amazing coldness (which is not a matter just of indifference, but rather of active hostility), the contempt and neglect they will show for the people of an outlying island, or for those living in the 'special' *buraku* (formerly a segregated social group now legally equal but still discriminated against). Here the complete estrangement of people outside 'our' world is institutionalized. In India there is a lower-class group known as 'untouchables', but although at first glance the Indian attitude towards a different caste appears to resemble Japanese behaviour, it is not really so. The Indian does not have the sharp distinction of 'them' and 'us' between two different groups.

Among the various Indian groups, A, B, C, etc., one man happens to belong to A, while another is of B; A, B, C, and so forth together form one society. His group A constitutes part of the whole, while, to the Japanese, 'our' is opposed to the whole world. The Indian's attitude towards people of other groups stems from indifference rather than hostility.

These characteristics of group formation reveal that Japanese group affiliations and human relations are exclusively one-to-one: a single loyalty stands uppermost and firm. There are many cases of membership of more than one group, of course, but in these cases there is always one group that is clearly preferred while the others are considered secondary. By contrast, the Chinese, for example, find it impossible to decide which group is the most important of several. So long as the groups differ in nature, the Chinese see no contradiction and think it perfectly natural to belong to several groups at once. But a Japanese would say of such a case, 'That man is sticking his nose into something else,' and this saying carries with it moral censure. The fact that Japanese pride themselves on this viewpoint and call it fastidiousness is once again very Japanese. The saying 'No man can serve two masters' is wholeheartedly subscribed to by the Japanese. In body-and-soul emotional participation there is no room for serving two masters. Thus, an individual or a group has always one single distinctive relation to the other. This kind of ideal is also manifested in the relationship between the master and his disciple, including the teacher and student today. For a Japanese scholar, the person he calls his teacher (master) is always one particular senior scholar, and he is recognized as belonging linearly to the latter. For him to approach another scholar in competition with his teacher is felt as a betrayal of his teacher, and is particularly unbearable for his teacher. In contrast, for the Chinese it is the traditional norm to have several teachers in one's life and one can learn freely from all of them in spite of the fact that they are in competition.

Thus, in Japanese society not only is the individual's group affiliation one-to-one but, in addition, the ties binding individuals together are also one-to-one. This characteristic single bond in social relationships is basic to the ideals of the various groups within the whole society. The ways in which interpersonal relations reflect this one-to-one linkage will be discussed at length in the next chapter.

2 The Internal Structure of the Group

In the foregoing discussion it has been shown that a group where membership is based on the situational position of individuals within a common frame tends to become a closed world. Inside it, a sense of unity is promoted by means of the members' total emotional participation, which further strengthens group solidarity. In general, such groups share a common structure, an internal organization by which the members are tied vertically into a delicately graded order.

Before I outline my analysis of this structure of internal organization I propose a set of effective concepts as the analytical basis of the following discussion. In abstract terms, the essential types of human relations can be divided, according to the ways in which ties are organized, into two categories: *vertical* and *horizontal*. These two categories are of a linear kind. This basic concept can be applied to various kinds of personal relations. For example, the parent–child relation is vertical, the sibling relation is horizontal; the superior–inferior relation is vertical, as opposed to the horizontal colleague relation. Both are important primary factors in relationships and constitute the core of a group's structure. It can be seen that, depending on the society, one has at times a more important function than the other and at times the two factors function equally.

If we postulate a social group embracing members with varoius different attributes, the method of tying together the constituent members will be based on the vertical relation. In other words vertical systems would link A and B who are different in quality. In contrast, a horizontal tie would be established between X and Y, who are of the same quality. When individuals having a certain attribute in common form a group the horizontal relationship functions by reason of this common quality. Theoretically, the horizontal tie between those of the same stratum functions in the development of caste and class, while the vertical tie functions in forming the cluster within which the upper–lower hierarchical order becomes more pronounced.

Let me illustrate these contrasting modes of social configuration with a simple example. A man is employed in a particular occupation and is also a member of a village community. In theory he belongs to two kinds of groups: the one, of his occupation (attribute) and the other of the village (frame). When the function of the former is the stronger an effective occupational group is formed which cuts across several villages; thus there is formed a distinct horizontal stratum which renders proportionally weaker the degree of coherence of the village community. By contrast, where the coherence of the village community is unusually strong, the links between members of the occupational group are weakened and, in extreme cases, the village unit may create deep divisions among members of the occupational group. This is a prominent and persistent tendency in Japanese society, representing a social configuration contrasting with that of Hindu caste society. For Japanese peasants, a village (local group) has been always the distinct group to which their primary membership was attached. In the Middle Ages when a large Buddhist temple formed a functional community embracing people of various occupations besides peasants belonging to its estate, it functioned as a kind of self-sufficient group, in which each occupational group was accommodated without functional linkage with any similar group outside the community. For example, carpenters of X temple rarely moved to another temple community and the situation was exactly similar to an occupational group in a modern institution. Throughout Japanese history, occupational groups, such as a guild, cross-cutting various local groups and institutions have been much less developed in comparison with those of China, India and the west. It should be also remembered that a trade union in Japan is always formed primarily by the institution, such as a company, and includes members of various kinds of qualifications and specialities, such as factory workers, office clerks and engineers.

In such a society a functional group consists always of heterogeneous elements, and the principle by which these elements are linked is always dominated by the vertical order. Certainly, in both kinds of social configuration, there exists a hierarchical order in the alignment of various groups. But when each occupational group is formed in such a way as to cut across various institutions it comes to possess an autonomy and strength which enable it to compete with other groups. In such a situation it is important that the ideology of the division of labour be sufficiently developed to counteract or balance the hierarchical ideology. However, when an occupational group of only small numbers exists within an institutional group, its members isolated from their fellows in other groups, there is a tendency for the hierarchical order to dominate the group and for the autonomy of the occupational group to diminish; the small, isolated segments become subject to the workings of the institutional group of which they form part. The result is the emergence of the vertical order in group organization.

1. The development of ranking

The vertical relation which we predicted in theory from the ideals of social group formation in Japan becomes the actuating principle in creating cohesion among group members. Because of the overwhelming ascendancy of this vertical orientation, even a set of individuals sharing identical qualifications tends to create a *difference* among these individuals. As this is reinforced, an amazingly delicate and intricate system of *ranking* takes shape.

There are numerous examples of this ranking process. Among lathe operators with the same qualifications there exist differences of rank based on relative age, year of entry into the company or length of continuous service; among professors at the same college, rank can be assessed by the formal date of appointment; among commissioned officers in the former Japanese army the differences between ranks were very great, and it is said that even among second lieutenants distinct ranking was made on the basis of order of appointment. Among diplomats, there is a very wide gulf between first secretary and second secretary; within each grade there are informal ranks of senior and junior according to the year when the foreign service examination was passed.

This ranking-consciousness is not limited merely to official groups but is to be found also among writers and actors, that is, groups which are supposed to be engaged in work based on individual ability and should not therefore be bound by any institutional system. A well-known novelist, on being given one of the annual literary prizes, said, 'It is indeed a great honour for me. I am rather embarrassed to receive the award while some of my *sempai* (predecessors or elders) have not yet got it.' *Sempai* meant for him those whose careers began and who achieved fame and popularity some time before he himself achieved them. Another example of the same sort is to be found in the statement made by an actress who had had great success in a film. On account of this success, she demanded that her company increase her guaranteed payment: 'I would like my present guaranteed payment (Y500,000) to be doubled. I think I am entitled to it, because actress Y is getting more than Y1,000,000 in spite of her being *kōhai* (junior: having started her career later) and younger than I. I have been an actress in this company for more than eight years now, you know.' For the Japanese the established ranking order (based on duration of service within the same group and on age, rather than on individual ability) is overwhelmingly important in fixing the social order and measuring individual social values.

A Japanese finds his world clearly divided into three categories, *sempai* (seniors), *kōhai* (juniors) and *dōryō*. *Dōryō*, meaning 'one's colleagues', refers only to those with the same rank, not to all who do the same type of work in the same office or on the same shop floor; even among *dōryō*, differences in age, year of entry or of graduation from school or college contribute to a sense of *sempai* and *kōhai*. These three categories would be subsumed under the single term 'colleagues' in other societies.

This categorization is demonstrated in the three methods of addressing a second or third person; for example, Mr Tanaka may be addressed as Tanaka-*san*, Tanaka-*kun* or Tanaka (i.e. without suffix). *San* is used for *sempai*, *kun* for *kōhai* and the name without suffix is reserved for *dōryō*.* The last form is comparable with the English usage of addressing by the Christian name.† But the use of this form is carefully restricted to those who are very close to oneself. Even among *dōryō*, *san* is used towards those with whom one is not sufficiently familiar, while *kun* is used between those closer than those addressed by *san*, former class-mates, for example. A relationship which permits of address by surname only is of a specifically familiar nature, not unlike the French usage of *tu*. Therefore, a man may also address very intimate *kōhai* in this way, but these *kōhai* will use the *san* form of address to him. In the case of professionals, within this pattern, a *sempai* is addressed as *sensei* instead of *san*, *sensei* being the higher honorific term, used of teachers by their students, and also of professionals by the general public.

It is important to note that this usage of terms of address, once determined by relationships in the earlier stages of a man's life or career, remains unchanged for the rest of his life. Let us imagine, for example, the case of X, once a student of Y, who, fifteen years afterwards, becomes a professor in the same department as Y and thus acquires equal status. X still addresses Y as *sensei* and will not refer to him as *dōryō* (colleague) to a

---

* *San* is the most general form of address, equivalent to Mr, Mrs or Miss. The differentiations here discussed apply only to men: women do not use such elaborate address terms in general social life, though in a special group (for example, among *geisha*) a similar pattern is found in the usage of different terms.

† The use of the first name in Japan is confined mainly to children. Among adults, it is employed only in relation to those who had close relations in childhood. One is addressed by the first name only by parents, siblings, close relatives and childhood friends.

third person. Y may address X as *kun*, treating him, that is, as *kōhai*, even in front of X's students or outsiders: Y has to be most broad-minded and sociable to address X as *sensei* in such a context (i.e. the English usage of Dr or Professor).

It may also be that when X is well known, but Y is not, Y may intentionally address X as *kun* in public in order to indicate that 'he is superior to X, X is only his *kōhai*'. It is the general tendency to indicate one's relatively higher status; this practice derives from the fact that the ranking order is perceived as ego-centred. Once established, vertical ranking functions as the charter of the social order, so that whatever the change in an individual's status, popularity or fame, there is a deeply ingrained reluctance to ignore or change the established order.

The relative rankings are thus centred on ego and everyone is placed in a relative locus within the firmly established vertical system. Such a system works against the formation of distinct strata within a group, which, even if it consists of homogeneous members in terms of qualification, tends to be organized according to hierarchical order. In this kind of society ranking becomes far more important than any differences in the nature of the work, or of status group. Even among those with the same training, qualifications or status, differences based on rank are always perceptible, and because the individuals concerned are deeply aware of the existence of such distinctions, these tend to overshadow and obscure even differences of occupation, status or class.

The precedence of elder over younger (*chō-yō-no-jo*) reflects the well-known moral ethic which was imported from China at a comparatively early stage in Japan's history. However, the Japanese application of this concept in actual life seems to have been somewhat different from that of the Chinese. An interesting example illustrates this discrepancy. When six Chinese *shōgi* (chess) players came to Japan recently to play against the Japanese, one thing that struck Japanese observers was the ranking order of the six players. In the account of their arrival carried by *Asahishimbun*, one of the leading Japanese daily newspapers, it was reported that Mr Wan, aged 17, the youngest of the six, stood fourth in order at the welcoming ceremony at Haneda Airport, and again at the reception party in Tokyo. The reporter went on to observe,

If we regard them according to the Japanese way of according precedence, Mr Wan, who is the youngest of them all and holds only *nidan* (second rank), should occupy the last seat in place of Mr Tsen, who though the eldest in years now takes the lowest place. They, however, take as the basis for position the order which resulted from the last title-match standings.

The Chinese are not always as conscious of order (seniority and rank, that is) as are the Japanese; they limit the effectiveness of seniority or rank to certain activities or situations and eliminate it from others. From what I have been able to observe, although the Chinese always appreciate manners which show respect towards those in a senior position, senior and junior might well stand on an equal footing in certain circumstances. The Chinese are able to readjust the order, or work according to a ranking established by a different criterion, by merit, for example, if the latter suits the circumstances.

In Japan once rank is established on the basis of seniority, it is applied to all circumstances, and to a great extent controls social life and individual activity. Seniority and merit are the principal criteria for the establishment of a social order; every society employs these criteria, although the weight given to each may differ according to social circumstances. In the west merit is given considerable importance, while in Japan the balance goes the other way. In other words, in Japan, in contrast to other societies, the provisions for recognition of merit are weak, and institutionalization of the social order has been effected largely by means of seniority; this is the more obvious criterion, assuming an equal ability in individuals entering the same kind of service.

The system of ranking by seniority is a simpler and more stable mechanism than the merit system, since, once it is set, it works automatically without need of any form of regulation or check. But at the same time this system brings with it a high degree of rigidity. There is only one ranking order for a given set of persons, regardless of variety of situation. No individual members of this set (not even the man who ranks highest) can make even a partial change. The only means of effecting change is by some drastic event which affects the principle of the order, or by the disintegration of the group.

It is because of this rigidity and stability that are produced by ranking that the latter functions as the principal controlling factor of social relations in Japan. The basic orientation of the social order permeates every aspect of society, far beyond the limits of the institutionalized group. This ranking order, in effect, regulates Japanese life.

In everyday affairs a man who has no awareness of relative rank is not able to speak or even sit and eat. When speaking, he is expected always to be ready with differentiated, delicate degrees of honorific expressions appropriate to the rank order between himself and the person he addresses. The expressions and the manner appropriate to a superior are never to be used to an inferior. Even among colleagues, it is only possible to dispense with honorifics when both parties are very intimate friends. In such contexts the English language is inadequate to supply appropriate equivalents. Behaviour and language are intimately interwoven in Japan.

The ranking order within a given institution affects not only the members of that institution but through them it affects the establishment of relations between persons from different institutions when they meet for the first time. On such occasions the first thing that the Japanese do is exchange name cards. This act has crucial social implications. Not only do name cards give information about the name (and the characters with which it is written) and the address; their more important function is to make clear the title, the position and the institution of the person who dispenses them. It is considered proper etiquette for a man to read carefully what is printed on the card, and to adjust his behaviour, mode of address and so on in accordance with the information it gives him. By exchanging cards, both parties can gauge the relationship between them in terms of relative rank, locating each other within the known order of their society.* Only after this is done are they able to speak with assurance, since, before they can do so, they must be sure of the degree of honorific content and politeness they must put into their words.

In the west there are also certain codes which differentiate appropriate behaviour according to the nature of the relation between the speaker and the second person. But in Japan the range of differentiation is much wider and more elaborate, and delicate codification is necessary to meet each context and situation. I was asked one day by a French journalist who had just arrived in Tokyo to explain why a man changes his manner, depending upon the person he is addressing, to such a degree that the listener can hardly believe him to be the same speaker. This Frenchman had observed that even the voice changes (which could well be true, since he had no knowledge of Japanese and so was unable to notice the use of differentiating honorific words; he sensed the difference only from variations in sound).

Certainly there are personal differences in the degree to which people observe the rules of propriety, and there are also differences related to the varying situations in which they are involved, with the result that the examples I have quoted may be felt to be rather extreme. Some flaunt their higher status by haughtiness towards inferiors and excessive modesty towards superiors; others may prefer to conceal haughtiness, remaining modest even towards inferiors, a manner which is appreciated by the latter and may result in greater benefit to the superior. And some are simply less conscious of the order of rank, although these would probably account for only a rather small percentage.

But whatever the variations in individual behaviour, awareness of rank is deeply rooted in Japanese social behaviour. In describing an individual's personality, a Japanese will normally derive his objective criteria from a number of social patterns currently established. Institutional position and title constitute

* See Chapter 3, particularly pp. 95–7 for detailed explanation.

one of the major criteria, while a man's individual qualities tend to be overlooked.

Without consciousness of ranking, life could not be carried on smoothly in Japan, for rank is the social norm on which Japanese life is based. In a traditional Japanese house the arrangement of a room manifests this gradation of rank and clearly prescribes the ranking differences which are to be observed by those who use it. The highest seat is always at the centre backed by the *tokonoma* (alcove), where a painted scroll is hung and flowers are arranged; the lowest seat is nearest the entrance to the room. This arrangement never allows two or more individuals to be placed as equals. Whatever the nature of the gathering, those present will eventually establish a satisfactory order among themselves, after each of them has shown the necessary preliminaries of the etiquette of self-effacement. Status, age, popularity, sex, etc., are elements which contribute to the fixing of the order, but status is without exception the dominant factor.* A guest is always placed higher than the host unless his status is much lower than that of the host. A guest coming from a more distant place is accorded particularly respectful treatment.

There is no situation as awkward in Japan as when the appropriate order is ignored or broken – when, for example, an inferior sits at a seat higher than that of his superior. It is often agreed that, in these 'modern' days, the younger generation tends to infringe the rules of order. But it is interesting to note that young people soon begin to follow the traditional order once

---

*Age and sex are superseded by status. For example, the head of a household, regardless of age, occupies the highest seat; his retired father retreats to a lower seat. Age will become a deciding factor only among persons of similar status. Status also precedes sex. It is well known that Japanese women are nearly always ranked as inferiors; this is not because their sex is considered inferior, but because women seldom hold higher social status. Difference of sex will never be so pronounced in Japanese thinking as in America, where classification (though not for purposes of establishing rank) is primarily by sex. I am convinced that in American society sex-consciousness predominates over status-consciousness, the exact opposite of Japan.

they are employed, as they gradually realize the social cost that such infringement involves. The young Japanese, moreover, is never free of the seniority system. In schools there is a very distinct senior–junior ranking among students, which is observed particularly strictly among those who form sports clubs. In a student mountaineering club, for example, it is the students of a junior class who carry a heavier load while climbing, pitch the tent and prepare the evening meal under the surveillance of the senior students, who may sit smoking. When the preparations are over it is the senior students who take the meal first, served by the junior students. This strong rank consciousness, it is said, clearly reflects the practices of the former Japanese army.

In the West the use of a regulated table plan is restricted usually to occasions such as a formal dinner party, when the chief guest is placed at the right of the host and so on. But in Japan even at the supper table of a humble family there is no escape from the formality demanded by rank. At the start of the meal everyone should be served cooked rice by the mistress of the household. The bowls should be served in order of rank, from higher to lower: among family members, for example, the head of the household will be served first, followed by his nominal successor (his son or adopted son-in-law), other sons and daughters according to sex and seniority. Last of all come the mistress of the household and the wife of the successor. The sequence of serving thus clearly reflects the structure of the group.

Since ranking order appears so regularly in such essential aspects of daily life, the Japanese cannot help but be made extremely conscious of it. In fact, this consciousness is so strong that official rank is easily extended into private life. A superior in one's place of work is always one's superior wherever he is met, at a restaurant, at home, in the street. When wives meet, they, too, will behave towards each other in accordance with the ranks of their husbands, using honorific expressions and gestures appropriate to the established relationship between their husbands. A leader in Japan tends to display his leadership in any and every circumstance, even when leadership is in no way called for. American behaviour is quite different in this particular: my experience among Americans is that it is often very difficult to discover even who is the leader of a group (or who has the higher or lower status), except in circumstances which require that the leadership make itself known.

A fixed seating order, particularly appropriate to and impressive in a Japanese-style room, extends also to the modern western-style room. At any gathering or meeting it is obvious at first glance which is the most superior and the most inferior person present. The frequency with which a man offers an opinion, together with the order in which those present speak at the beginning of the meeting, are further indications of rank. A man who sits near the entrance may speak scarcely at all throughout the meeting. In a very delicate situation those of an inferior status would not dare to laugh earlier or louder than their superiors, and most certainly would never offer opinions contradictory to those of their superiors. To this extent, ranking order not only regulates social behaviour but also curbs the open expression of thought.

In such manners we can observe how deep the ranking consciousness operates among Japanese. In this regard, I recall Tibetans, the pattern of whose everyday manners is very similar to that of the Japanese, in that they employ gestures and varying degrees of linguistic honorifics according to the difference in recognized ranks between speakers. However, I observed that when Tibetan scholars sit for a debate they completely renounce all difference of rank and rank equal to each other. I was told that even the Dalai Lama is no exception to this practice. Japanese scholars, on the other hand, never escape from the consciousness of the distinction between *sempai* and *kōhai*, even in the case of purely academic debates. It is very difficult for a Japanese scholar to disagree openly with a statement of his *sempai*. Even a trifling opposition to or disagreement with the *sempai*'s views involves an elaborate and roundabout drill. First, the objector should introduce a long appraisal of the part of the *sempai*'s work in question, using extremely honorific terms, and then gradually present his own opinion or opposition in a style which will give the impression that his opposition is insignificant, being afraid to hurt his *sempai*'s feelings. The ranking of *sempai* and *kōhai* thus stifles the free expression of individual thought.*

The consciousness of rank which leads the Japanese to ignore logical procedure is also manifested in the patterns and practices of daily conversation, in which a senior or an elderly man monopolizes the talk while those junior to them have the role of listener. Generally there is no development of dialectic style in a Japanese conversation, which is guided from beginning to end by the interpersonal relations which exist between the speakers. In most cases a conversation is either a one-sided sermon, the 'I agree completely' style of communication, which does not allow for the statement of opposite views; or parties to a conversation follow parallel lines, winding in circles and ending exactly where they started. Much of a conversation is taken up by long descriptive accounts, the narration of personal experiences or the statement of an attitude towards a person or an event in definitive and subjective terms unlikely to invite, or to reach, a compromise. The premises underlying thesis–antithesis are parity and confrontation on an equal footing which will develop into or permit the possibility of synthesis. Because of the lack of a discipline for relationships between equals, the Japanese do not practise these three basic steps of reasoning and must overcome great odds in order to advance or cultivate any issue brought under discussion. Hence most conversations are intellectually dull, emotionally enjoyable to the speaker, with a higher status, rather than the listener, with a lower status. Too seldom is the speaker a good entertainer who can lead his listeners to join a worthwhile game.

In particular, a junior takes every care to avoid any open confrontation with his superior. Such attempts lead to the point that a flatly negative form is rarely employed in conversation:

* The ranking of *sempai* and *kōhai* is determined by the year of graduation from university, which is always one of the narrow group of leading universities.

one would prefer to be silent rather than utter wo
'no' or 'I disagree'. The avoidance of such open and
tive expression is rooted in the fear that it might
harmony and order of the group, that it might hurt the feelings
of a superior and that, in extreme circumstances, it could involve the risk of being cast out from the group as an undesirable
member. Even if there are others who share a negative opinion,
it is unlikely that they will join together and openly express it,
for the fear that this might jeopardize their position as desirable
group members. Indeed, it often happens that, once a man has
been labelled as one whose opinions run contrary to those of
the group, he will find himself opposed on any issue and ruled
out by majority opinion. No one will defend him in any circumstance.

Thus, the expression of opinion in a group in Japan is very
much influenced by the nature of the group and a man's place
in it. At a group meeting a member should put forward an
opinion in terms that are safe and advantageous to himself,
rather than state a judgement in objective terms appropriate
to the point at issue. This is why a junior member will rarely
dare to speak up in the presence of his superior. Freedom to
speak out in a group is determined by, as it were, the processes
of human relations within the group; in other words, it goes
according to status in the group organization.

The consciousness of ranking order among members of a
group also distorts the modern formal procedure of a committee
meeting. The chairman's authority and rights are easily overruled by a committee member whose place in the seniority system is higher than the chairman's; at the same time the chairman
would not dare to put forward a decision without the consent
of the most senior member of the committee. The status of the
chair is not well established in Japan. One of the most appropriate examples is offered by the procedures of the Japanese Diet.
The variety of confusions and deadlocks in committee meetings
in Japan seems to derive in the main from the lack of authority
to preside (and the techniques of such authority) on the part
of the chairman, and from the failure to recognize the authority

of the chairman by the participants. Order is always restored after such confusion or deadlock by resort to a procedure which reflects more faithfully the ranking order of the participants.

Ranking consciousness has become an important cause of frustration to ability-conscious personnel directors in modern enterprises. There is much evidence on this matter which comes in for much discussion among those concerned. I have come across several concrete cases during the preparation of this book. The rank of an employee is determined first by his educational qualifications and then by the date of his entry into the company. This latter is not a standard prescribed by management but is rather something that is firmly fixed in the consciousness of the workers themselves. In many large companies each year's entrants form themselves into a club. Such 'year clubs' have the function of pointing up the distinction in rank between those with long experience and newcomers within the company, and help further to entrench the seniority system. If a man from a certain year's intake is promoted his fellows will be considerably disturbed and will even demand similar promotion on the grounds of equal suitability. If the person promoted is a junior the demand will be even more insistent. This surprisingly strong consciousness of rank is difficult for even the most efficient management to overcome. The Japanese consciousness of 'I can do it, too' is stronger that that found anywhere in the world; objective rating of one's own ability is minimal. These factors are, I think, directly related to the institutionalization of the ranking system. No matter how assiduously the company attempts to introduce and sponsor objective methods, those methods will not be successful. As a result, management is driven to promote several individuals from the same year-group, taking care to avoid creating any appreciable gap between them. Hence, the many assistants and acting ranks in every sector of employment in Japan.

It can be said that the bigger and older the enterprise (with the attendant higher stability and density in the employee group), the stronger the institutionalization of rank. Conversely, in small and medium-sized industries and in newer enterprises it is more easy to make the shift from seniority pay to merit pay, or to a system of promotion by capability. The rigid seniority system is often regarded as the 'traditional' system, which should be moved towards and changed into a 'modern' pattern. However, it is interesting to note that this rigid system is a more recent development, not to be found during the earlier period of Japan's industrialization, which appeared in the later and more sophisticated stages of industrialization. If we examine the history of individual enterprises the evidence is almost without exception of a similar process of continuous movement towards the development of a more rigid ranking order.

Some of the new, successful post-war enterprises, such as Sony, for example, or Honda, used to pride themselves on their modern democratic management; but after they had reached a certain stage of development, when the establishment had grown larger and achieved stable success, there gradually developed within such firms this rigid seniority system, in the same pattern as is to be found among older, larger, established enterprises. Some Japanese interpret this phenomenon as evidence that a company has 'matured', for it is a general truth in Japan that the larger the size and the firmer the establishment of an institution, the greater the inclination among its personnel to develop an internal ranking order and to evolve a bureaucratic pattern. This phenomenon may be universal, but the form it takes in Japan is unique.

Not only does the strength of this ranking transcend differences of occupational type; in addition, year-group consciousness admits of no concern for the usual occupational classifications. This is because, from the beginning, a man is employed not in a specific job but rather for whatever type of work the company shall determine for him. The usual practice is for an individual to do a variety of different work in succession. Thus, from the standpoint of both management and employee, there is no firmly defined 'occupation' system. One might theorize that the strengths of these horizontal (occupational) and vertical (rank) relationships are inversely proportional.

Whereas there is in Japan no notable horizontal group consciousness within such groups as executives, clerks, manual workers and so on, there is instead a strong departmentalism constructed along the functional vertical tie. It may group together a section head and his subordinates; in a university department, for example, the professor, assistant professor, lecturer, assistant and students are linked together in a vertical relationship. The professor is closer to his lecturer and assistant (who are most probably his former students) and to his students than he is to any of his fellow professors.

There are many consequences of such vertical organization. Frequently, for example, it is not the man who is the most obviously capable but rather a more pliable person who is elected as the chairman or the head of any collective body. The claims of the more capable man are often passed over because of the fear among other members that he might work for the advantage of his own group, which, in fact, given circumstances normally prevailing in Japan, he is quite likely to do.

This kind of orientation in human relations in Japan contrasts sharply with that of other societies. In America and again in England, for example, teaching staff in a university or executives in a firm form a more functional group based on 'colleague' identification. Minor differences of individual rank tend to be ignored; in place of rank, there are sharply defined groups – assistants or students against professors, clerks or workers against executives, for example. Among Indians, this kind of group consciousness is even more pronounced. For example, members of the IAS (Indian Administrative Service) develop a caste-like feeling which sets them apart from other workers in the administrative institutions. A deputy commissioner feels much closer to his colleagues in the IAS in other offices or in other parts of India than he does to the immediate subordinates in his own office who are not members of the IAS. I was surprised to find that a group of IAS men who met by chance on their way to a conference were able to strike up an immediate companionship, regardless of differences in age and the year in which they passed the IAS examination. This could never occur among their Japanese counterparts. Among Japanese, a difference of even one year at entry and minor divergencies in the stages of promotion may well create a feeling of unease which would preclude any companionship. An Indian IAS man informed me that a consciousness of difference of status may develop between men whose length of service differs by more than seven years. A difference of this degree would affect promotion and the nature of the work. However, even this difference is not as great as that which separates IAS and non-IAS men. These senior men are like the elders of a caste, always concerned for the welfare of their own people.

Although a year-group, or a set of class-mates of a school, are recognized in Japan, such groups are the outcome of the ranking system itself. In other words, such group consciousness exists because of the ranking system and is not that of a horizontal group created primarily for the enjoyment of comradeship. Rather, it demarcates clear lines of rank within the picture of the total group or institution. One of the tests of the effectiveness of human relations within a year-group, in contrast to a vertical group, can be seen in the effectiveness of letters of introduction. A Japanese writes a letter of introduction very readily even without much sense of responsibility, on the basis of 'knowing the man'. Hence, it is difficult to be sure whether a letter of introduction will be effective or not. In normal circumstances little can be expected from an introduction given to a class-mate of similar rank unless there is some particularly close friendship or some common and important interest involved. On the other hand, a letter of introduction from a distinguished senior man to his subordinate is very effective. It will ensure proper, even unreasonably generous, treatment, quite irrespective of the subordinate's views of the bearer of the introduction, and of the latter's status. The vertical line is much more effective than the horizontal line.

In face of these forms of human relations and the vertical-group organization which naturally derives from them, group consciousness based on a common attribute, such as that to be found among college professors or labourers, is inevitably very weak. The consciousness of like qualities, enfeebled by this internal structure, is further weakened by a lack of contact with similar people outside one's own group and by the tendency towards the building of social groups into frames. And here, again, in place of the consciousness of the same occupation, is the ever-present consciousness of the same 'household'.

2. The fundamental structure of vertical organization

The ranking order which produces delicate differentiations between members of a group develops firm personal links between superior and subordinate. Such relationships form the core of the system of a group organization. A group structure based on a vertical line of this strength is demonstrably different from one based on a horizontal line.

The structural difference between group X (vertical) and group Y (horizontal) can be demonstrated in the following way. In Figure 1 the three points, a, b and c represent the members of each group, assuming that each group is made up of the same number of individuals. In Y these three points form a triangle or a circle, but in X the base of the triangle is missing or very weak. If there is any link the nature of the relationship b–c is quite different from that of a–b or a–c. Hence the structure forms not a triangle or a circle but an inverted V (hereafter indicated by the sign ∧). Although a, b and c constitute a group, it is not necessary that each of the three shares a common requirement as the basis of forming a group. The group is formed by the accumulation of the relations a–b and a–c with a as the focal point. In contrast, in the case of Y, a, b and c share the same attribute, which is the basic requirement for the formation of the group; thus the attribute of membership is very clear and becomes the basis of group formation. It is immediately obvious to an outsider whether he may join the group or not. In the case of group X there is no such obvious rule governing membership, so that any outsider, provided he can become acquainted with and accepted by one of the members, may join; access to the group is rather a situational and personal matter, the context of which may differ case by case. The addition of a new member to the group involves no alteration to the place of any existing members, he being placed on the lowest rank.

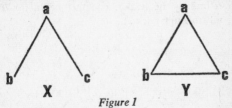

Figure 1

But in group Y the participation of a new member would affect everyone in the group. However, once his entry is effected, he will be in the same position as all the other members. In group X there can be unlimited variation in the modes of incorporation, and the outsider can enter easily, but it is an inflexible structure in which the individual member cannot change his relative position within the organization. The individual's group participation is regulated by his established relation to a given group member, which is by itself the fixed basis for his incorporation into the group. On the other hand, in Y in theory any individual can take the place of any other within the group, and a new member is able to stand on the same footing as all the other members. These structural differences are demonstrated by the position and function of *a*. In Y the position of *a* (and of each group member) can be modified in accordance with changes in other members. Y group's organization can continue without the existence of *a*, because *b* and *c* are linked. But in the case of X, because the constituents are all linked with *a*, the pivot of the organization, the absence of *a* leaves the other members unable to build or sustain the group's organization. Herein lies an important problem concerning the characteristics of group leadership.

If we examine the relationship of a group to its leader we note first that in X, while it is not impossible, it is very difficult to change leaders. In addition, the leadership is always restricted to one individual. In this X structure it is impossible for two or more persons to stand in parallel or equal positions. Thus the several relationships linking the leader to other group members do not necessarily have the same attributes. In Figure 2 the relation linking the leader *a* to member *d* (or *a* to *g*) is operative only through *b* (or *c*).

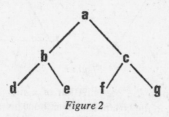

Figure 2

As has been said, the group is based on the accumulation of relationships between two individuals: the group in Figure 2 consists of the relationships *a–b*, *a–c*, *b–d*, *b–e*, *c–f* and *c–g*. The relationship between two individuals of upper and lower status is the basis of the structural principle of Japanese society. This important relationship is expressed in the traditional terms *oyabun* and *kobun*. *Oyabun* means the person with the status of *oya* (parent) and *kobun* means with the status of *ko* (child). In Figure 2, *b* is the *kobun* of *a* (*oyabun*), and at the same time he is the *oyabun* of *d*. One person may play more than one rôle. The traditional *oyabun–kobun* realtionship took the form of patron and client, landowner and tenant, for example, or master and disciple. The expressions are still used today, although more informally. *Oyabun* may be one in a senior position at a man's place of work, with whom has grown a close personal relationship over the years. The essential elements in the relationship are that the *kobun* receives benefits or help from his *oyabun*, such as assistance in securing employment or promotion, and advice on the occasion of important decision-making. The *kobun*, in turn, is ready to offer his services whenever the *oyabun* requires them. In the case of a funeral of a man of higher rank, for instance, his juniors rush to the household to help in the preparations and even contribute more than the dead man's kinsmen or neighbours.

Most Japanese, whatever their status or occupation, are involved in *oyabun–kobun* relationships. There was an excellent example in a recent election for the Governor of Tokyo. When the successful candidate, a well-known professor of economics, was asked to stand as the joint candidate of the Socialist and Communist Parties his first act was to run to his former teacher (*oyabun*), a very well-known economist almost eighty years old, to take advice on whether he should accept the offer or not. The press took this action as natural and anticipated the meeting of the two professors; the following day's newspapers carried pictures of the meeting and stressed the importance of the opinion of the *oyabun* professor. The *oyabun–kobun* relationship comes into being through one's occupational training and activities, and carries social and personal implications, appearing symbolically at the critical moments in a man's life. Indeed, the *oyabun* plays the rôle of the father, as the term suggests. And it is by no means exceptional for the *oyabun* to play a more important rôle than the father.

The degree to which this relationship functions may vary considerably case by case. Various elements, such as the *oyabun*'s ability, his status and personal attraction and the relative weakness of the *kobun*, contribute to strengthen the relationship. Some *oyabun* may have a broad range of *kobun*, possessing wide influence and power, while others may have only a few *kobun*; or a man may not merit the term *oyabun*, being no more than a senior (*sempai*). It is the same with the *kobun*: some would not be able to name a particular man as *oyabun*, but even in such cases there is likely to be some particular senior (*sempai*) with the flavour of *oyabun*, whom, for instance, it would be hard to refuse when some form of service was requested. There may be more than one such *sempai*, but normally there is a particularly close relationship with one of these. The tendency to distinguish one particular *sempai* as *oyabun* becomes more prominent as the *oyabun–kobun* relationship becomes more effective. A man may change his *oyabun*, but such a change in itself indicates the weakness of the relationship. And there may be, of course, the exception who has no *oyabun* (but may or may not have *kobun*), or refuses to recognize the authority of his *sempai*. Such a man, the lone wolf (*ippiki ōkami*), is powerful and active but reluctant to conform. Since an *oyabun* is normally shared by equals, the refusal to recognize an *oyabun* also results in ostracism from the group sharing an *oyabun*. Whatever variations may be found in individual cases, it may be said that groups in Japan are formed by the multiplication of a vertical relation between two individuals. Thus the individual locus is determined informally within the network of such a relationship.

Now we must return to Figure 2, to discuss the mechanism of the network forming the group. If the link between *a* and *b* breaks, the ties linking *d* and *e* to *a* are automatically cut: *a*'s control over *d* (as over *e*, *f* and *g*) is possible only through *b* and *c*. In the *a–b* relationship, to the extent that *a* controls *b*, he can extend his control over *d* and *e*. Consequently the core of the group structure is in the *a–b*, *a–c* relationships. Break these and, inevitably, internal disruption of the group will follow.

In X therefore the existence of *a* (and the *a–b*, *a–c* links) has incomparably more importance for the maintenance of the group than it would have in Y. No matter how strong the unity, no matter how 'happy the group' (to use a Japanese expression), the sudden removal of the leader is a severe blow, and automatically brings a 'household rebellion' (the Japanese expression for an internal struggle).

It is said that the greatest battle weakness of the former Japanese army was the disruption that followed when a platoon leader was killed. A platoon that lost its organizational pivot by the death of its lieutenant easily degenerated into a disorganized mob, committing gross errors of judgement. In the British and American armies there is no such disruption; a substitute platoon leader quickly steps out from the ranks, and control of the platoon remains undisturbed until there is only one soldier left. Although it may seem that the group organization triangle in Japan has a line across the base, this tie functions hardly at all; without a, a relation between b and c cannot be maintained. Further complexities arise because b and c seem then to be ready to develop antagonistic ambitions which can splinter the group into factions.

Herein, then, lies the supreme importance of the rôle of the leader; he is the holder of legitimate status and is also the outstanding personality, able to synthesize the members and suppress antagonisms among them. The leader's absence from his men, even though only temporary, may give rise to increased antagonisms among them. The Buddhist sage, Hōnen (1133–1212), recognized this, perceiving that, when he was absent, his disciples would fail to stay on amicable terms with each other, and would bicker among themselves. So, facing his followers, he said, 'You shall not stay together, but each go his own separate way.'

In group structure of this nature a change of leadership leads to a very critical period for the continuance and stability of the group. In many cases groups split into a number of small and hostile segments after the death of the leader. The chaos thus created can rarely be repaired internally. The difficulty in installing a new leader lies in the personal relationship between him and the rest, rather than in his capability for the work. First of all, the position of the leader-to-be is in a way legitimized if his acceptance as leader does not destroy the relations already existing in the group. Legitimacy is based on seniority (not necessarily of age but of years of service in the group): the most senior man is also very probably the man highest in rank after and closely linked with the leader, since the group hierachy is formed according to the order of entry into the group. If there is more than one man in such a position the most senior in age would become the first candidate for succession to the leadership. Such a succession scheme would certainly be affected and perhaps be disturbed by particular circumstances and elements in a given case, but it remains the procedure most acceptable to all the members of a group.

Secondly, in order to exercise leadership a man must have a personal côterie directly attached to him, which forms his stronghold. The leader-to-be should not only be the most senior man with direct links to the leader but also a man with a considerable number of *kobun* directly attached to him. His predecessor's *kobun* are not always willing to remain attached to the new leader, but may take up a position in competition with him. For this reason a son might sometimes fail, or find it difficult, to succeed to his father's office: in fact, it often happens that the most senior man attached directly to the former leader takes the succession in place of the son (see pp. 113–14).

In view of the structure of the group, however, whether the successor is the leader's son or his most senior subordinate, and whether he is a man of ability or not, a leader who has newly succeeded is handicapped in the exercise of his leadership in comparison with the first leader of the group. The first leader of the group (when the group is young, i.e. founded by this leader) possesses decided advantages in terms of group structure. He stands far beyond comparison with the members of his group, in that he became leader by his own efforts and merit, so that all group members are *de jure* and *de facto* his *kobun*, and this makes him drastically different from subsequent leaders.

There have been many examples in the post-war period of successful enterprises beginning on a very small scale and growing, under the leadership of the founder, to be leading companies with upwards of 10,000 employees. National, Sony and Sanyō lead in the electrical field, Honda and Idemitsu in motors and oil respectively; all are still under the control of the founder, whose exercise of leadership is sharply distinguishable from that of those who have succeeded to the presidency of older and more traditional enterprises.

It is the general pattern that such enterprises lose some of their vitality under a succeeding leader; in the second generation there develops a bureaucratic stability which may readily spawn factions and blunt the earlier initiative of the pioneer. If an enterprise is not firmly established before the death of its founder-leader and has difficulty in deciding on his successor internal disorder and dispute may well lead, as has regularly happened, to bankruptcy and disintegration. One of the most eminent directors of an industrial enterprise has stated that it is the duty of the manager to prepare his successor, and if this duty is neglected true management is not possible. In Japanese thinking it is the leader's duty, therefore, before death or retirement, to prepare and indicate a successor acceptable to the members of the group. The preparation of a successor is vital also to a political party. The survival or disintegration of factions (*habatsu*) within Japanese political parties depends primarily on the existence of a suitable successor after the death of the *oyabun*.

In the group structure exemplified in X in Figures 1 and 2 (p. 43 and 44) it should be noted that it could disintegrate not only from *a*'s (the leader's) death or absence but also from instability in the *a–b* or *a–c* links. Such instability may occur if the leader fails to sustain a strong influence and an immediate subordinate seizes the opportunity to increase his own power. For instance, if *b* has amassed numerous followers and commands enough power to manipulate group life he would normally be frustrated in that he cannot overrule *a* or become leader as long as *a* remains in the group. Nor does *b*, a frustrated, capable subordinate, have any opportunity to establish a partnership with the leader, for their original positions as leader and subordinate cannot be changed. The legitimacy of the leadership has its base in the historical formation of the group. If *b*'s power grows to the point where it can shake this existing order developments usually occur on the following lines:

Noting *b*'s restiveness, *c* may sense his opportunity and, drawing closer to *a*, may encourage tension in the *a–b* relationship, eventually creating a critical and unstable situation which will lead to a crisis. Then even while *a* is still in the position of authority, an internal split may occur. This would lead to complete catastrophe, from which nothing could be salvaged. But *b* could in no circumstances co-operate with *a* or *c* in such a power struggle. This is not because the participants are emotional or petty-minded; it is a consequence of the inherent structural situation, which does not allow two or more individuals to be equal, or more than one to lead.

There are two alternative solutions of such a catastrophe. In one a (usually taking c along) is exiled from the group (in Japanese parlance, the '*head-clerk-taking-over-the-store*'). In the other solution b pulls out his 'family and retainers' and forms a new, independent group, a process which is called *fission*. After c has been excluded, whether f and g follow c or whether they form a new attachment to b, d or e, and thus become part of the b faction, depends on the relative strength of c–f or c–g relations. Among these peripheral members there are various possibilities for adjustments to the new situation. Since these members are on the fringe of the group and cannot be part of the nucleus, they are free to make a new alignment because the group's structure allows each member the possibility of the attachment of new members. The structure of Λ, however, operates so effectively in the area close to the nucleus that, regardless of his actual power, it is almost impossible for a new participant to break into the nucleus.

The structure of X thus reveals an instability which always involves the risk of fission. Indeed, in may cases fission is taken for granted at a certain stage in the growth of the group. This may be called 'amicable' fission, for fission is expected by the leader as well as by other members when the subordinate acquires enough strength to be independent. Nevertheless, the splinter group does not always maintain amicable relations with the original core. Often it may become a competitor, unless the leader of the original group can control or bind it in some way, or unless the second group is still so weak as to expect help from the original body.

The best illustration of such a process is the traditional manner of establishing new agricultural households or new mercantile shops by a second son, an adopted son, or servant or tenant of the original household or shop. Among modern occupations a similar process operates, for example, among lawyers and doctors. It is customary for a young lawyer or doctor who has just finished training to enter one of the well-established offices, under the guidance of the head of the office, and after some years' work to set up his own independent office.

Especially capable men would not remain in their chief's office, since, as has already been pointed out, there would be no opportunity to advance to a partnership. Indeed, the ambition of any such young capable Japanese would be to have an independent office or practice of his own. There is not a system of partnership in the sense that obtains in Britain or America, for it is very difficult for Japanese to form a partnership on western lines. Even though a relationship may be styled 'partnership', closer observation always reveals that *de facto* it is a senior–junior structure, which becomes obvious, particularly in the process of decision-making. Even such a 'partnership' is likely to become unworkable when it has more than three members.

A system based on a vertical relationship works effectively when the junior member is content with his position under his senior. But when a man of oustanding ability who makes distinguished contributions to his group develops dissatisfaction with his senior, the mechanism of the group does not allow any outlet for the expression of such dissatisfaction. As will be explained later, the Japanese system does not have a clearly marked division of labour, nor is the individual role of each member of a group distinctly determined. Any returns from the individual's contribution are enjoyed by the group as a whole, with the resultant prestige attributed to the leader; meanwhile, the capable man who has made significant contribution stays as one of the junior members. His boss and his colleagues may be well aware of his distinguished contribution, but they take it for granted that it should be a matter of profit to them to have such an able member in their group.

Thus, unless a man is in the top position, he rarely has a chance to enjoy public appraisal and prestige. It is this social mechanism that leads many Japanese to be obsessed by the feeling, 'I am *under* someone', and to be controlled by the desire to obtain the headship, regardless of their capability and personality. In order to achieve one's goal, there are only two alternatives – first, that a man waits for his turn, or secondly, that he leaves and establishes his own group. A very capable man often finds it difficult to remain in his group. When his contribution is very obvious to anyone outside the group and his reputation brings him outside popularity it very often happens that he incurs his colleagues' jealousy and hostility. Any popularity or outside reputation should be enjoyed by the group as a whole, not by the individual; no individual popularity should exceed that of the senior or boss. The Japanese ethic puts high value on the harmonious integration (*wa*) of group members. The defiance of individual quality and achievement, which derives from the group structure, often leads a capable man with no immediate chance of attaining leadership to leave the group and establish himself independently.

In that the internal structure of the group does not allow for any easy change in the relative locus of the individual member or permit him to be the immediate superior of subordinates directly attached, the possibility of fission or disruption is latent and the development of factions is a constant potential feature. The size of an actual functional core of a group is always small. These circumstances lead to two well-known Japanese features – the formation of intra-group factions and the development of a number of independent similar groups within the same field of activity, these groups possessing no means of controlling or accommodating each other.

Japanese society offers numerous examples of these features. The Liberal–Democratic Party, for example, contains nine major factions (*habatsu*), and the same characteristics are to be found in the Socialist and Communist Parties. The Zengakuren (All-Japan Federation of Students' Self-Governing Associations), which was formed in 1948, has split into several distinct groups, each with its own doctrine. The number of factions and the degree of coherence of these groups change constantly. In the course of such inter-movement much time and energy are spent in fights between competing factions. The strength of the group as a whole (such as a political party) is based on the balance of competing powers among the most dominant factions (frequently three in number).

The coherence of a group as a whole comes first from the history of segmentation from a common founder: units within a group are related and therefore differentiated from others or outsiders. Secondly, perhaps a more important factor in group coherence is the external situation; if each faction feels itself surrounded by so-called enemies the group can maintain a stability based on a balance of the powers and the hierarchical order of its factions, in spite of competition and antagonism between these factions.

The enlargement of a group is always directed towards the attachment of new members or groups vertically. Groups are linked by the head of a weaker group either to the head or one of the members of a stronger group; there is never a horizontal link between the two heads. This process leads to the creation either of a single huge institution or of a distinct group within which a large number of institutions or groups are organized hierarchically. In Japan any kind of large organization always assumes a bureaucratic structure; there is a complete absence of caste-like group organization. In consequence of this structural orientation of group formation there grows that picture of contrasts – a number of minor, similar institutions, on the one hand, and on the other hand, a single huge institution or a group of institutions – that characterizes Japanese society today.

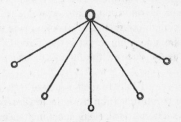

Figure 3

Whatever their size, Japanese groups share common structural characteristics. Regardless of the size of the whole group, the functionally effective core is fairly small, usually of one or two dozen members, a size which enables each member to have direct contact with all the others, who can be organized on two or three levels, including the leader on the top level; thus members on the lowest level do not stand too far (i.e. through too many levels) from the leader. The ideal type of effective group is that shown in Figure 3, which is organized on two levels, with all members linked directly to the leader. When a group becomes larger, with an increased number of levels, the effectiveness of the entire system tends to decrease, and a functional core develops at each level.

The workings of the system prohibit a man at a lower (or on the lowest) level from communicating directly with someone at the highest level in the organization. In the case of the leader at the top of the organization, the voice of those in the lower sectors is transmitted only through the men linked directly to him, and he has great difficulty in acquiring first-hand information. It is considered against the rules for a man at the lower end to speak to or ask for an appointment directly with a division head or director; he should not leapfrog his section head, his immediate superior, for such action would bring loss of face to his section head and would be regarded as an insult to the status of the division head or of the director. An opinion or a good idea from a man at a lower level may reach the top, but only through the legitimate route, by way of his immediate superior. There is an appropriate example of a university president refusing to consider a suggestion made by an ordinary professor, while accepting exactly the same proposal a few days later from the dean of the faculty to which the professor belonged.

These factors contribute to inefficiency of organization, in the matter of poor communication from the lower sectors to the top and between sections. However, such inefficiency is perhaps more than balanced by the extreme efficiency of communication from the top to the lowest level. Indeed, the swiftness by which the members of a group can be mobilized from the top in Japan is not paralleled in any other society. The secret of such swift action and the source of the high level of group energy seems to lie in the nature of the core of group organization, based on the relationship between two immediately linked men. The golden rule is that the junior man should invariably carry out any order from his immediate superior, for this immediate link between the two men is the source of the existence of the junior man in the organization. Hesitation or refusal constitute a violation of the system, even if the execution of the order takes a man outside his assigned rôle, for what is important is the working of the vertical system, rather than the nature of the work or the formal assignment of rôles. The prompt acceptance of an order by a junior predisposes his senior in his favour, and the accumulation of such give-and-take relations further strengthens the bond between the two and contributes to the mobilization of the entire group.

However, at the same time this highly involved relationship between the two men again entails the phenomenon of 'the creation of groups within a group', the sectionalism from which Japanese organizations regularly suffer. This precludes horizontal relations. It is difficult for a horizontal link or balanced co-operation between sections to function in Japan. The equal balance of powers between peers or collaboration between two equally competing groups is almost non-existent in Japanese society, for when there is more than one faction within a group one will dominate. The existence of equally competing powers is a most unstable situation in Japan; stability always resides in imbalance between powers where one dominates the others.

A *de facto* coalition of equally strong factions is unlikely in Japan, for one of the factions is always invested with disproportionate weight. On this basis the leader mediates between opposing factions in order to arrive at group consensus, and will appeal to the weaker faction to concede its point 'for the sake of my face' – that is, for his standing and reputation; and if the leader's face is saved, so is that of the opponent. Given such group structure and the use of emotional appeals, a majority opinion readily emerges. Thus, though the issue itself may never be subjected to logical examination, the group can reach agreement to act on a generally accepted decision. General agreement prompts readiness to act, and if a recalcitrant minority adamantly resists concession, radical action might finally be taken by which this minority could be made outcasts from the group. As a result, the dissidents tend always to be the same minority members, regardless of the issue. This tendency often entails radical and futile activity on the part of the minority group; its views are always ineffective, and it always ends up the loser in decision-making. The Japanese are pleased to call this method of decision-making 'democratic', by which they imply the entitlement of the majority to rule over the minority. In Japanese group dynamics the stability of the group, if it consists of more than two factions, can be maintained by imbalance in the power and the weight of the factions, and at the expense of minorities.

As, even within one group, it is difficult to establish a co-operative link and balance between two sub-groups, it is almost impossible to create a horizontal link between two or more independent groups. When two leaders collaborate, each bringing his followers with him, in an attempt to form a new combined group, even if both segments had previously been parts of a common larger group and had split away from it, it is impossible for them to come together again. The process is illustrated in Figure 2. If, because of the death of a, the separate groups b and c should join forces while preserving their original internal structure (thus attempting to create a horizontal link between them) the attempt would be doomed to failure, for a link cannot be made between them as long as their respective internal structures remain unchanged. If they had developed originally as separate groups, even though their activities and aims were similar, they could not be merged into one group unless they managed to find a single legitimate leader acceptable and suitable to both groups. The merger of two groups can take place only if one absorbs or dominates the other, or if a leader emerges satisfactory to both; this latter is indeed very rare. Even when both groups profess to be 'hand in hand', this is usually merely a slogan and does not reflect the actual condition.

We should note here that Japanese history knows no instance of oligarchy. Nor have the political parties of modern Japan ever had recourse to the device of the coalition. One party always dominates the others, and there has always been a single leader, legitimate and acknowledged by all factions, though not necessarily a man of power.

Even when two groups have the same aims and courses of action, it is still extremely difficult for them to work together. This leads to situations which it is impossible to explain by any common-sense point of view. The atomic-bomb memorial incidents in recent years are a case in point. In 1963, for example, the Communist and Socialist Parties (including Sōhyō) were not able to join together for the performance of the memorial ceremony, with the result that the ceremonial hall became the stage for their open quarrels. And more recently, memorial services for the victims of the hydrogen-bomb test at Bikini Island were held in Yaizu by two competing groups (The Peace Association of Japanese Religious Men and Sōhyō) at the same place but at different times. Their unseemly wrangles distressed both the Mayor of Yaizu and the bereaved family, who were torn by their social obligations to attend both functions, and the two competing groups gained little beyond the contempt of the local people and the general public. In spite of such reactions from outside, groups still destroy themselves by such deadly internal group-versus-group wrangling. Meanwhile, the outsider begins to question the groups' social responsibility. It is for these reasons that political cliques (*habatsu*) are so vulnerable to attack on ethical grounds; from the outside, their concern seems to be preoccupied with interpersonal relations inside factions, interrelations of factions-within-a-faction and interfactional disputes. Thus, the goals of the organization tend to be deflected by the everyday procedure of group life.

The industrial field is not exempt from the effects of internal group structure. 'Reorganization of industrial enterprises', by which is meant the merger of individual enterprises of similar kinds, has become one of the main national efforts to offset the invasion of foreign enterprise into Japan which followed the recent adoption by Japan of an economic policy aimed at an international free market. For Japan's particular industrial situation it is certainly profitable to establish larger enterprises by a combination of already existing enterprises; this enables the resultant larger enterprise to compete in the international market and to increase profits proportionately by avoiding unnecessary domestic competition and double-investment. Directors of many larger enterprises who are aware of the theoretical advantages of the merger find, however, that their hopes face great obstacles that can arise from interpersonal rivalries, among the directors and executives of the enterprises involved as well as among the managers and managerial staff within an individual enterprise. There are innumerable instances which reveal the development of such difficulties from the group structure I have described. Here I would like to discuss only two examples, one representing a successful merger and one representing a failure.

The first example concerns three large enterprises which be-before the war formed one *Zaibatsu* group (see also pp. 101–2) called Mitsubishi Heavy Industries Company. It separated into three entities in 1950: Mitsubishi Japan Heavy Industries Company, New Mitsubishi Heavy Industries Company and Mitsubishi Ship Manufacturing Company. Long and complicated negotiations were necessary before a successful merger was achieved. The basic reason for their success seems to have been a happy blend of personal relations among the directors. According to the economic critic, Seki Tadatake, editor of *Zaikai* (Business World), the key figure was Mr S. Fujii. Mr Fujii had become director, after having been the president, of New Mitsubishi Heavy Industries Company after the sudden death of the company's former director. He was respected as *sempai* by the other two directors, was known as a man of great achievement and was far from being an egocentric personality. He was, in addition, a former colleague of the presidents of the two other companies; the three men had entered Mitsubishi at almost the same period and had worked together, so that it was not difficult for the other two directors to become co-directors under Mr Fujii. The success of the merger of these three companies derived from the fact that it destroyed none of the internal structure of the companies and caused no disruption of the traditional ranking system which has always been particularly prized by Mitsubishi men.

In another instance, while the top personnel agreed to the merger, it failed because of the opposition of executive members of one of the companies. Asahi Beer Company and Sapporo Beer Company, formerly a single enterprise called Dainihon Beer Company, divided into two soon after the war. The two directors were on good terms, having been together in Dainihon Company, and they were in favour of merging. If and when the merger was completed the director of the merged company was to be Mr T. Yamamoto, director of Asahi Beer Company. Mr Yamamoto was known as despotic, while Mr Matsuyama, director of Sapporo, was known as a democratic manager and the pioneer in Japan of scientific techniques in beer production. When a news story disclosed the plan the whole of the executive staff of Sapporo Beer Company joined to oppose the proposal, saying that they would not work under the despotic director. They were happy enough under the present democratic director, and although they were aware of the benefits of the merger from the point of view of the business advances it would bring, they felt that the problems of day-to-day organization were of more importance and relevance. Because of this strong opposition, the attempt was cut short only two days after the plan for the merger was announced in the press. Following this experience, the director of Sapporo said the idea of a merger 'will never cross my mind again'. One might ask why he did not force his men to agree with the merger, by exercising the advantages of his popular leadership. However, as I shall discuss later, the power of a Japanese leader is much restricted by group consensus. If he had forced a merger against the will of his employees he would have risked losing their devotion and collaboration.

From the above discussion two negative characteristics of group structure X can be deduced as follows: (1) the group is always under the risk of internal fission; (2) it has a crucial external weakness of not permitting co-operation between groups. On the positive side, when the group is functioning at its best the power and efficiency of X in concentrating and mobilizing its members' energies can exceed that of Y, since in X the ties binding individuals together are emotional and stable. It follows, however, that the efficiency of X is open to impairment through accidents or ambitions which upset its balances of power.

It is demonstrable that the informal hierarchy and the factions which develop among a group's members (the invisible organizations discussed above) overlap and supersede an institution's formal administrative (visible) organization. In firmly established institutions, such as long-founded companies and governmental organizations, the instability and disintegration of informal groups are well compensated for by the institutional frame itself. Even when the informal hierarchy is deformed or destroyed, individual members still remain within the frame; and even while its efficiency is lowered, the group can preserve itself by means of the formal administrative organization. The institutional frame indeed fulfils the important function of keeping the members together, whatever factions are found within it; and, since members are classified primarily by the institution, whatever internal rivalries they may feel, they realize that they are all in one boat racing with other boats. It goes without saying that the degree of effectiveness of an institutional frame (the coherence of its members) is heightened when the institution possesses wide prestige and an important rôle in the society.

In cases where a group has no constant frame with a formal institutional administrative system, such as a company or a village, the function of the hierarchical organization tends to become more important. This occurs with groups such as political parties or underground organizations; in such cases the informal vertical organization itself becomes the group's *de jure* organization. A prototype of this kind of organization is to be found in *iemoto-sei* (literally, 'origin of the household system') in the traditional arts such as *nō*, flower arrangement, or tea ceremony. *Iemoto* – the head of the school – stands at the apex of the organization and the succession to his position is normally hereditary. Innumerable vertical line links originate in the office of *iemoto*, through the master-disciple relationship, and in the case of the older and more successful schools the Λ shape network often covers almost the whole of Japan. It is a matter of some surprise that these older schools have retained the same organization over several centuries and that some of them still flourish today. The *iemoto* attracts not only the highest prestige but also the greatest economic advantages; he can collect fees for a certificate of proficiency from individuals who are linked to him indirectly in the hierarchical organization, as well as fees for direct teaching. The system thus not only serves to transmit artistic techniques, but also has a wider and more effective economic and social function.

The relationship between different schools in the same artistic field is poor. In *nō*, for example, there are five major schools, each with an organization quite independent of the others but of exactly the same structure and function. Members of different schools hardly ever perform on the same stage, although they share texts basically the same, and an actor will not attend plays given by schools other than his own. Even if the programme contains plays by more than one school, members of the audience belonging to one of the schools normally leave their seats during the performance of the other school. Not only does an artist not mix with members of other schools in the same field; he will also not change his master within the same school. The *iemoto* system demands that every individual retains the vertical line once established between master and disciple. Such a behaviour pattern fits nicely into the structural principle of the organization. One realizes here the far-reaching structural implications of the golden rule of Japanese ethics – 'No man can serve two masters.'

The basic pattern of the organization is inherited to a certain degree, though on a smaller scale, by the modern professionals, such as modern artists, scholars, lawyers, etc. The internal composition of associations of lawyers in Japan, for example, is clearly based on vertical relationships, although their activities rest primarily on an individual basis, rather than on employment by an institution. The vertical relationship found between individual advocates is created by former teacher–student and *sempai–kōhai* relationships in the same university, or master–disciple and *sempai–kōhai* relationships in the advocate's office where they were articled at the beginning of their careers. Through such vertical relations the group manifests a lineage-like organization. It is interesting to learn that for these advocates each group is conceptualized as a village community and, in fact, the traditional Japanese term used for these groups is *mura*, a village. At a committee meeting consisting of representatives of each group, when an important issue comes up and a representative is not able to give a spot decision, he will say, 'I withhold my decision until I can refer it back to my *mura*.' A faction within a political party is similarly termed *mura*. A candidate new to politics in an election for the House of Councillors was asked to which *mura* he belonged. He showed his ignorance of the jargon by answering, 'I come from Tokyo,' meaning that he was a native of Tokyo. What it was intended to discover, of course, was to which faction he belonged. The primary community (significantly termed *mura*) of contemporary Japan is thus a faction within a professional or occupational group.

Without either 'frame' or 'vertical links', it seems to be almost impossible for the Japanese to form a functional group. In fact, in Japan it is very difficult to form and maintain the sort of voluntary association found so often in western societies, in that it does not have the basis of frame or existing vertical personal relations. There were many attempts to organize voluntary welfare groups after the Second World War on the pattern prevalent in America. Most of these have failed to function in the manner of their American counterparts, because of lack of organizing personnel, active participation on the part of members and social recognition by the general public. In face of such unexpected difficulties, most organizers approach the Government for formal or informal support, which enables the establishment of an effective network at national level and brings social recognition.

Such difficulties face not only voluntary groups but also the development of a new local community in the suburban areas of large cities. Municipal authorities, as well as sociologists, etc., have produced a series of plans for the development of what they call 'community life' (another concept imported from America), in general without success. As I see it, the formation of such groups, presupposing, as they do, horizontal links between members, cuts across existing groups based on work place. Committed to groups based on their primary business activities, they are reluctant to contribute money or time to local residential groups. Surveys by sociologists of local communities reveal that the most likely basis for the formation of a local community organization is the catchment area of a primary school; contacts through a Parent–Teacher Association afford more opportunities for access and association, but, even so, there is difficulty in the way of embracing households with no schoolchildren.

The tight coherence of the Japanese village community is often interpreted as that of a local group; but my point is that the traditional village is the group in which the members conduct their vital economic (i.e. agricultural) activities, and is a closely knit sociological entity through the generations rather than a mere residential group. When villagers move to urban areas place of work and residence are separated and precedence is given to the place of work, which is their community (the village, as they see it), rather than to the local residential group. As in the case of the advocates and politicians, their 'village' is their professional 'lineage' group, not the neighbourhood in which their houses are actually located. Former practice in Japan was that the voting in national elections went by a kind of village 'card vote', village members agreeing to support a candidate recommended by a local boss: in recent years, however, it has become prevalent for an enterprise (with its satellites and sub-contracting companies) to cast a block vote for a chosen candidate, with unions and management normally in agreement on the choice. In such cases a local community cannot match the authority and functional strength of a company as a group. Single-group participation is thus manifested in the lack of development of new local communities in urban areas in Japan. (See also p. 131)

Though they may fail to develop a new local community, many new urban residents join new religious groups, of which the most successful today is Sōka-gakkai, with an estimated membership of three millions. Sōka-gakkai is a kind of patron group attached to a particular Buddhist temple belonging to the Nichiren sect and all members are laymen. Surveys of the group reveal that membership is drawn mainly from the upper sector of the lower strata of the urban population, and conversion to the group usually occurs within two or three years after the move into the city from the countryside. Active group members, on the whole, give precedence to group participation over membership of associations based on their place of work. Conversion seems to occur before a man becomes an active and influential member of organizations based on his place of work. It is not without significance that Sōka-gakkai is organized along vertical lines, to which the movement itself has given the name *tate-sen* (literally, vertical lines). The *tate-sen* are the result of the extension of direct lines built between two individuals. The individual's place along the *tate-sen* is determined at the time of his conversion to Sōka-gakkai, and this *tate-sen* eventually reaches up to the president at the apex, cutting across areas and other institutions. The organization within the top sector of the ultra-loyal staff mirrors Japan's former military system. The astonishing success of these new religious groups, which have grown so large and so rapidly, seems to be attributable mainly to their system of vertical organization.

In society not all groups experience in the same degree the effect of the functioning of the organizational principle. One might discover a group which does not have as its organizing principle the vertical organization described in this essay; however, it might well be, in such a case, that the group was formed very recently and had not had sufficient time to mature as a corporate body, or the group may not be a really functional corporate group to which its members are primarily attached.

But if it is, after all, a well-matured functional group the size of the group will be found to be small, perhaps less than two dozen members, or it may consist of fairly homogeneous members of similar social and economic standing who know each other thoroughly (as in some hamlet communities where families have lived together for generations). In such exceptional cases the group can be thoroughly democratic, with no rigid hierarchy of internal structure. Or there might be a group of persons having similar educational background and training but different fields of specialization; in this case a high degree of specialization on the part of each individual member helps to establish a distinctive locus which hinders the development of subordinate or subjugate relationships with other members and promotes mutual interplay while maintaining individual autonomy.

Even in such exceptional circumstances of group formation, a group which has neither internal hierarchical order nor the superior–inferior type of human relations still demands that its members give unilineal participation and develop their own closed community. Again, such uniformity, balance of power and democratic mentality among the members of a group would not be preserved when the group becomes larger. If a homogeneous community adds members from outside itself or experiences external influences internal differentiation is the normal outcome. In the case of a group based on individual specialization the addition of members with identical or similar specializations will result in the development of vertical relationships, since, as has been said earlier, no two persons can occupy the same rank.

Hence the existence or absence of vertical hierarchy within a group and its degree of institutionalization depend on the situational factors of its formation. What is most important is that in Japan a group inevitably and eventually develops the vertical type of organizational structure. Further, an organizational structure based on the vertical principle appears more pronouncedly in well-established, large institutions with a higher degree of prestige. This is the source of the stability of the organization, which seems the major strength of the Japanese system.

It is worth observing that in Japan any group which achieves success and increases in size while also developing in stability always follows this same structural pattern. The degree of function of vertical relationships may differ according to groups; and in some groups there may exist no obvious vertical relationship. However, the inference is that, the stronger the functioning of the group, the more likely it is that its human relations have been built along these lines. This structural principle is latent in all social groups in Japan.

The strength of this structure lies in its effectiveness for centralized communication and its capability of efficient and swift mobilization of the collective power of its members. The importance of its contribution to the process of modernization is immeasurable. It has been noted above that this structure served to underpin Japan's post-war economic growth. Yet the vertical structure known as *oyabun-kobun* has been looked upon by Japanese as well as by Americans as a 'feudal' or 'familial tradition', as something pre-modern, operating against the interests of modernization. Such a view fails to see the real structural significance, for the *oyabun-kobun* relationship and the modern bureaucratic system embody the same structural orientation, and the differences are not of quality but of degree – for while the former involves and recognizes more of the personal elements, the character of the latter is more impersonal.

3. Qualification of the leader and interpersonal relations in the group

In the structure of the group, as demonstrated in the previous section, the qualification of the leader rests primarily on his locus within the group, rather than his personal merit; the loyalty of other members towards the leader also derives from their position as subordinate to him. The most significant factor in the exercise of the leadership is the personal ties between the leader and his immediate subordinates. Strong, functional personal ties always derive from the informal structure. In a given situation this informal structure may or may not coincide with an institution's formal and visible administrative organization. The man in the office of leader in the formal organization who has subordinates tied informally to another leader outside his formal organization has a very difficult time in Japan. Though on the surface his subordinates appear loyal and subservient, his orders are often not carried out behind the scenes and he is sometimes betrayed. He may be able to establish new personal ties through the formal organization, but this becomes more and more difficult as his career advances. For everyone tends to establish personal ties at a comparatively early stage in his career, and personal ties established in the earlier days tend to supersede those developed at a more advanced stage: the earlier the establishment, the stronger the function.

In fact, a man moving to a position of high responsibility tries his best to bring in his *kobun* as his formal subordinates. It is well known and recognized among Japanese doctors that a change of director of a large hospital involves the replacement of the great majority of those in subordinate posts: the top man moves in or out with his *kobun*, his subordinates in an informal structure. It goes without saying that, on gaining the premiership, the leader of a political faction similarly moves in with his *kobun*. This tendency is strengthened when the nature of a group's activities calls for close teamwork; it is in a group of this nature that the characteristics of Japanese leadership are most clearly demonstrated.

The vertical personal relationship is more dynamic in character than the horizontal relationship. Protection is repaid with dependence, affection with loyalty. Because this is not an equivalent exchange, it tends to enlarge the emotional element beyond that to be found in horizontal relations, and to make for easier control of the actions of individuals. This relationship does not bind the subordinate only; it also binds the leader who, though he may often appear to be able to exercise a great deal of power, sometimes of a despotic type, in fact, in comparison with leaders in other societies, finds his authority checked and controlled at a great many points. As I have said, the loyalty of a subordinate to his leader is highly regarded in Japanese ethics, and is often forced by the leader, but in practice the cost of receiving loyalty is high. It is governed largely by the relative quality of the relation between the leader and the subordinate, indications of which may be found in the political, economic or emotional elements. Normally all these factors are present, although the emotional factor has particularly important connotations.

The emotional sympathy felt by the leader towards his subordinate is expressed in the term *onjō-shugi*, or 'paternalism', and always presupposes a sympathetic appreciation of his men. The subordinate's opinions and wishes will enter deeply into his considerations. In fact, the better and greater the leader, the more strongly is this tendency revealed. In other words, the wider the chief's perceptiveness and permissiveness, the better followers will he have. The characteristic of super-subordination inherent in this leadership is also demonstrated in what is called *ringi-sei* (a kind of a consensus system) that is well developed in Japan. Superiors do not force their ideas on juniors; instead, juniors spontaneously lay their opinions before their superiors and have them adopted. This practice is also to be found in allowing a bureaucratic organ to administer policies.

One of the characteristic features in the operation of this system is that the weakness of the superior may be covered by his subordinates, and *vice versa*. In this system it is not essential for the superior, including the man right at the top, to be intelligent. In fact, it is better if he is not outstandingly brilliant. If his mind is too sharp and he is excessively capable in his work the men below him lose a part of their essential function and may become alienated from him. To counterbalance the dependence on the leader on the part of his followers, it is always hoped that the leader, in his turn, will be dependent on his men. The leader must have some weakness for which his men are always ready to compensate or provide support. Having established a firm relationship in this manner, the followers are always eager to understand and co-operate with the leader's ideas and actions.

Such characteristics demanded of the Japanese leader accord nicely with the seniority system. Alternatively the pattern of the relationship between the leader and his subordinate may have developed through the custom of recognizing the seniority system. For the group certainly can maximize its function when it possesses an outstandingly able leader followed by devoted subordinates, and such devotion of subordinates can be gained only when the leader is an exceedingly able and perceptive man. The functioning of the relationship between the leader and his subordinates, described above, offers an adjusting mechanism when an ordinary man occupies the top post because his turn in the seniority system has come. By the seniority system the highest office is always occupied by the most senior man in the group. Seniority is based on length of service in a group or an institution, rather than on a man's actual age. This system affords little chance to the younger man to occupy a post of high rank, for the top post or the office of the leader in Japan is normally occupied by an elder, who sits very comfortably in the office and receives very high social prestige in spite of any lack of the necessary ability. This is obvious when we compare Japan with other societies. It would be inconceivable, for example, for Japan to have a prime minister in his forties – Kennedy's age when he became President. Leaders of the Liberal–Democratic Party, which has a comparatively long history, are mostly in their seventies, and it is from these that Japan has chosen her prime ministers since the late 1940s. A comparatively young leader only arises from a newly formed group; the leading members of the Kōmeitō (the youngest political party in Japan, backed by the Sōka-gakkai) are in their forties.

In academic circles responsible positions are occupied by professors who are nearing or have reached retirement; in the older academic establishments scholars in their forties are considered not to be old enough to take an office, such as the head of a department or association, director or chairman of a committee, where there are members in their fifties and sixties.

In general, the peak of a man's social and political activity is reached in the years after fifty, as he approaches the age of retirement. In industrial fields, a man does not normally become a director or president until he is over sixty, at least in older established companies. It was a newsworthy event when a man was made the director of Japan Electric Company in his early fifties. Even if his work is highly distinguished and internationally known, a young scholar is rarely promoted to a professorship, in that he is still too young by traditional counts. The election of a President of Tokyo University in his middle forties also made news. The general attitude to this unusual appointment was that the critical nature of the situation (the revolt of radical students) justified the choice; but there were latent feelings of uneasiness, especially among older faculty members. Thus it appears that such disregard of established practice occurs in an emergency or at times of great social and political change. It should be remembered that during the Meiji period, when the process of Japan's modernization began, many young men in their thirties and forties occupied top posts in various fields. However, once the system became established, and after positions of power had been handed from one generation to the next, the possibility of an event such as the appointment of a younger man over the heads of his elders became much more restricted. It has been said that during the War even the commander-in-chief of a major campaign was appointed in accordance with the existing hierarchical order of seniority, which derived simply from the year of graduation from the Army or Navy College.

Under such a system it is to be expected that much frustration must exist among capable younger members, particularly among those in their middle years with considerable experience and achievements in their respective fields. A man thus frustrated may leave to form his own independent group; but if he is a member of a group which has influence and is in a position of advantage he would lose considerably by leaving and thus he tries instead to increase his authority from within the group. In this case the system itself can offer an outlet for his frustration. As has been said, the relationship between leader and subordinate is one of mutual dependence. When a leader depends very heavily on his subordinate the latter can readily encroach on the domain of his leader. Indeed, a subordinate often *de facto* carries the work of his leader, and in such a case he can extend his latent power over the entire group, while making use of his leader's name. He would benefit himself far more in this way than if he himself were to take over *de jure* leadership of the group, for within the ∧ shape organization he is not in a position to influence his collaterals and their subordinates. In Figure 2, for example, if *b* takes *de jure* leadership *a* and *c* together with *c*'s subordinates are reluctant to carry out his orders, and he is able to mobilize only his own subordinates *d* and *e*. There are many cases in which the subordinate plays a greater rôle than that officially assigned to him. In this sense, a Japanese leader offers a considerable degree of freedom to his subordinates. Hence the ranking or position of the group members does not always reflect the real working procedure, and indeed it is often difficult for an outsider with little knowledge of the group to perceive who is responsible for what business.

However, the ranking has paramount importance in terms of the external activities of the group, since this is the order by which the entire Japanese social system works. However more influential and capable than his leader a subordinate may be, he must never treat his leader in terms other than that of great deference in the presence of a third party; he must save his leader's face. In private dealings between the two the subordinate may behave as he likes, and the leader may show considerable weakness in face of his capable subordinate; in fact, the nature of the relationship and behaviour is not dissimilar to that often found between Japanese husband and wife. In the event, in many cases the subordinate status may be far from intolerable, compensated as it is by such a relationship behind the public scene. However, this state of 'home affairs' should not be exposed to outsiders. As a result, rank still carries significant social implications as a support of the social order.

The general tendency in Japan is to accord prestige to status rather than to real merit. This encourages a man, whatever his capabilities, to wish to reach the top. In fact, very ordinary and quite ineffectual people reach the top, simply because they are the most senior in the organization. As a result, it often happens, for instance, that an interviewer finds himself unexpectedly disappointed on meeting a man at the head of an institution in Japan, for he discovers him to be a very ordinary person and can see no evidence of the special ability that would be appropriate to the office.

Some American executives visiting Japan have expressed surprise that so many Japanese directors are unable to explain the details of their own enterprise. They rely cheerfully on their beloved and trusted subordinates to run the business; of much greater concern to them is the maintenance of happy relations among the men, for in this they believe lies the key to business success. One would have to search widely in Japan to find the company, so common in the West, run by only one or two men at the top while the employees act as simple tools. In such a pattern employees are easily replaceable, and the lines of responsibility between manager and employee are clearly drawn. In the Japanese pattern there are no clear-cut spheres or divisions of responsibility between the manager and his subordinates, and the entire group becomes one functional body in which all individuals, including the manager, are amalgamated into a single entity.

The foregoing discussion highlights one of the important features of the leader–subordinate relationship in Japan – the leader is a part of the group organization. He does not have his own independent domain separable from the rest of the members of his group. In fact, the Japanese language has no term for the word leadership; to express the concept, one has to fall back on terms describing the *oyabun-kobun* relationship. The leader is expected to be thoroughly involved in the group, to the point where he has almost no personal identity. There are examples of a director whose company is facing bankruptcy or who has taken over an almost bankrupt company refusing to take a salary and giving his services free until he has achieved success for the company.

In the Tokugawa period the feudal system made no clear differentiation between the personal or family property of the lord and that of his retinue or of those on the estates he controlled. The lord had no personal estate which he directly controlled and managed. When the estate suffered from a poor harvest or from shortage of land as a result of overpopulation his personal expenditure was cut and his men were ordered to be thrifty. The lives of the lord and his retainers were intimately linked, so as to form a single household economy. Today, as then, an effective demonstration of leadership informs employees that even the leader shares hard times with them.

Even though a leader might appear despotic, he could not have reached his position unless he were aware of, and had fulfilled, this qualification. He could only exercise a taste for dictatorship to the point where he could still hold his men emotionally and fulfil their expectations. Indeed, some subordinates would admire his despotic behaviour, in contrast to the warm regard and care he might show to them on informal occasions, and even rude behaviour would be taken as a reverse expression of his affection. The quality of such a leader is quite different from that of the dictator known elsewhere.

Be that as it may, variations in leadership in terms of the leader's methods of expressing command – in despotism or democracy, or simply idiocy – is not the really important point. Such differences are individual and conditional. The important point is that, because of the ambiguities in the field of function of the leader and the subordinate, the range over which the leader exercises authority is determined by the relative balance of abilities and personalities which the leader and his subordinate bring into a given group.

More than anything else, the qualification of the leader in Japanese society depends upon his ability to understand and attract his men. No matter how great his wealth and power, how brilliant his talent or what type his personality, if a man is unable to capture his followers emotionally and glue them to him in vertical relationships he cannot become a leader. Consequently it may be that Japanese soil cannot grow a charismatic leader, or, to put it in other words, a leader may exercise his charisma only through immediate personal relations. The strength of personal ties inhibits the attraction of a leader who possesses only charismatic qualities. In fact, the enduring Japanese image of the leader is not that of Napoleon but always that of Oishi Kuranosuke, leader of the famous Forty-Seven Rōnin.*

The functioning power of the group depends not so much on the leader's own ability as on his skill in charming extremely talented subordinates by his personality, his artfulness in synthesizing the group and his ability to direct all the talent at his disposal. Those who are regarded as great leaders are always extremely charming. The acts of their followers are dependent not on formal orders from the chief but on the personal charm he exerts in direct human contact. The phrase 'He shone his face upon me' has more importance than can be judged rationally. It is said that soldiers who shouted 'Banzai to the Emperor' and

---

*Since Oishi was an extremely paternalistic leader, he enjoyed such complete devotion from his forty-six retainers that they left their families and set out on a course which would end in the suicidal deed (*harakiri*), in order that they might assist the leader's revenge on his own master. This has been the most popular story among the Japanese: it is said that, even in the worst times of depression, if this play were shown at the theatre it was always sure of a full house. The Forty-Seven Rōnin reveal in extreme form the ideal personal relationship (always in terms of superior–inferior) in Japanese eyes. The story bears some resemblance to a love affair. In Japan there is no love story comparable in popularity to the Forty-Seven Rōnin. Men so much involved in such a relationship have little room left for a wife or a sweetheart. In traditional morals the ideal man should not be involved in an affair with a woman. I think that if he were involved to such an extent in this kind of man-to-man relation there would seem to be no necessity for a love affair with a woman. His emotions would be completely expended in his devotion to his master. I suspect this was the real nature of *samurai* mentality, and to a certain extent the same may be true of the modern Japanese man.

prepared to die were always filled with warmth and loving respect, saying as they gave their lives, 'This is what the commander asked us to do.' The commander's great concern was to hold his men emotionally; otherwise he would be of no effect in the battle. It was essential even for his own protection; the emotional dedication to his commander on the part of the soldier would lead him to sacrifice his life readily for the safety of the commander.

In business the crucial quality in managers and other men at the top is personality, and there is probably no country where the personality of the manager presents such a problem both to those immediately concerned with him and to the public in general. Many articles in Japanese newspapers and magazines discuss the personality of this and that manager and the relations between employer and employee. The following are recent examples:

'*Shain* (those who staff the company) are not *shiyōnin* (personal servants of the employer). They are collaborators in the business. Together with the employer they are collaborators working for the success of the business. This relationship is not explained fully by a term such as workers-and-manager.' (Quoted from remarks by the Director of Ricoh Watch Company, known to have made rapid advances since the present director took over.) In this company a counselling office was established in 1963; ex-directors act as counsellors to employees in all manner of personal problems.

The Canon Company, well-known for the production of cameras, is also famous for its so-called 'Familial Management', an idea initiated by the present director who believes a healthy and happy home is the source of his employees' energy for work. Recently a system of offering prizes to employees, called 'Prize for a Happy Home', was established. The prize is given to those employees who have worked with perfect attendance and punctuality and without accident for five years. At the ceremony the employee is accompanied by his wife. (Here we see a nominally American influence in terms of open consideration of one's home or wife; but in the philosophy of the management, it is entirely non-American.)

In the Japanese context these cases are viewed as representative of 'modern and progressive human management' and the personality of such directors is greatly admired.

There is a high degree of personal involvement between manager and employee. It is customary for the director or department head to attend the employee's wedding ceremony as a go-between. Indeed, a director spends considerable time away from his office on such occasions. On the other hand, on the occasion of a funeral in the director's family his secretary and subordinates help with the preparations for the ceremony and the reception afterwards, while his relatives and friends are received as guests and relieved of all tasks.

The manager's problem is not a new one. Since the early years of industrial Japan he has had to come to grips with the concept that 'the enterprise is people' and with problems concerning people. Do American managers worry to this extent about their employees? Is such thinking even necessary in America?

If the tie between management and labour is so strongly emotional, even in modern enterprises, there is certainly no question about it in the boss-system of the underworld; there are those who will go as far as to kill themselves for the sake of the boss. According to the principal of a juvenile detention home, the reason that children who have once had a taste of the underworld keep returning to it and finally return to it for good is probably that in the underworld they receive a love and appreciation from their *oyabun* that cannot be had from any correctional institution nor even from foster-parents. For weak people the emotional security deriving from the strong leader–follower relationship creates a peaceful world.

It is significant that the new religious sects that proliferated after the war based their group organization on an emotional, vertical line, mediating direct contact through a hypnotic leader. The 'vertical line' in Sōka-gakkai's forced conversion and the 'parent–child' relationship in Risshō-kōseikai are prototypes of this structuring. Beguiled by these familiar elements, the believer is brought neatly into the organizational net and can sink into the secure feeling of 'I am not alone any more: in this world they understand me, I understand them; we are the same people.' It would appear that the strength and essence of these religious groups lie in sociological and psychological factors rather than in any aspect of dogma.

The vertical relationship represented in the form of ∧ becomes itself the vital structural core of functional groups which have either no particular frame of institution or only a very weak one. The group stakes its life on the very personal relation of ∧; of necessity this organization is accentuated and grows more uncompromisingly rigid. The politicians' world and the under-world are prototypes of such groups; others appear in such areas as commercial fishing groups that are dependent on un-stable small-scale capital (where the fisherman's boss is the 'capitalist' for the group, the lead boat and dependent boats), and carpenters' associations, etc. These types of associations have been criticized as 'backward' or 'feudalistic', and have been given the pejorative labels of 'boss system' or 'party faction'. Yet the same principle operates also among people with progressive ideas – university professors specializing in western economics and society, those at the top in giant corporations and so on.

Among examples of intellectuals associated in this way are the academic research groups which flourished in post-war Japan. They were very different in a number of ways from, for instance, Italian and French research groups within my experience. To begin with, a European research group is not usually named after a particular university or association, nor are all its members necessarily from the staff of the group leader's university or from his graduate students. In Europe the group leader usually chooses, from the whole breadth of the field, the specialists most appropriate to the research group's purposes and the group is constructed by invitation. Consequently, people may join who had previously known the director only slightly. Once the con-tract between the group head and the members is made, the relationship between them remains firm until the research is finished; within the realm of the work, the director's orders are followed absolutely. For example, no matter how famous a photographer might be, once he has become a member of the group, he will take pictures as the director indicates (even when the director is younger and less well known than the photographer). However, even during the research period, group members are completely free in off-duty hours. There is never any reason to consult the director's wishes about any action unrelated to the work, although within the limits of the task the director can make the group conform to his wishes in order to achieve his purpose.

On the other hand, when Japanese academic research bodies form heterogeneous groups with similar contractural patterns they almost invariably blunder. Where they do not fail completely, work proceeds inefficiently because all energies are expended on emotional human relations and the operation does not go at all smoothly but becomes a tremendous burden. Even professors of leading universities quarrel in front of outsiders and foreigners, with the result that they give the country a bad reputation for bickering. No matter how famous the individual members or how large a grant they have received, the work progresses badly. Generally this sort of group splits up, whereupon the director invariably becomes the object of malicious carping.

For the purpose of scientific research, nothing works so effectively in Japan as a group made up of a senior professor as leader and members selected only from his own followers. Such a team can achieve its goal no matter how meagre its funds or how dismal the environment. The group members have the 'beautiful, positive quality' (in Japanese terms) of sparing no effort for the sake of their leader, while from the other side there comes the sympathetic consideration of a leader who offers an affection not just limited to the feeling that 'they're good fellows'. In this relationship, of course, the director has power, but his authority is much less real than that of his European counterpart. In consequence, a talented, scholastically pre-eminent Japanese leader may be unable to carry out the work as he wishes: he must accept his men's opinions, even when inferior to his own, in such a way as to enhance the men's importance. The need is emotional rather than rational – in that the leader should spur his men's incentive. The leader's *raison d'être* is not so much to direct the project nor to develop his own research, as to serve as a pivot for human relations and keep the peace. The research group is a *Gemeinschaft* entity, 'everyone's group', 'our group', not the director's personal following.

But a European research group is the leader's property; it is a *Gesellschaft* unit in which group members do no more than play their assigned rôles in order to complete the director's work. At the end, when the group finishes its work and disperses, the group leader and the various members may well lose all affinity. In Japan the ties resulting from an act of co-operation have a strong chance of lasting a lifetime. Only in such warmth of relationship can they hope to complete their task successfully.

It is my conviction that in Japanese society, at least at present, this type of personal relationship is the group's driving force and brings greater success than any other type of group organization. Anyone with experience in directing or co-operating with groups of people in any kind of operation would adopt it out of necessity. If the participants have not previously worked together over a long period of time there is little chance of success unless they are fitted smoothly into relationships. The source of trouble is, of course, human relations, particularly those developing emotional overtones. If the individual members among themselves, or the group members and the leader, do not get along well not only will everyone begin to neglect his work but some will even abandon their jobs. When his needs are not completely met, it is a favourite practice of the Japanese to put his leader in difficulty by saying, 'That's the end. Here's my resignation' (sometimes in earnest, sometimes as a bluff). In thus causing discomfort to a superior they enjoy a certain egotistical satisfaction. Above and beyond any effects of provocation or lack of a common goal or sense of responsibility for the accomplishment of the work, one detects this strongly emotional tendency in the Japanese, and senses the importance he attaches to the emotional content in human relations. Not only can this emotionality prevent fulfilment of a contract, but one might say that fundamentally the concept of contract does not exist at all and this applies to those performing the work and those commissioning it.

The Japanese always use an existing structure of vertical personal relations for the organization of any inter-institutional or inter-professional group, such as an organizing committee of a large convention of the kind that requires the co-operation of experts from various fields. First, an invitation goes to a set of top-ranking men in each respective field, and these form a kind of honorary committee. The members of such a committee are mostly senior in years, with their time well occupied by their work; they are thus not necessarily available for or suited to assist in the actual work of an organizing committee, but they do have significant power and influence to mobilize helpers in their respective field. The second stage is the formation of the real functional committee from a set of middle-aged experts who have accepted the request of their respective leaders in the honorary committee. It is this committee that performs the actual work. A group formed in this way has a certain weakness in that it lacks an internal ∧ shape structure. Nevertheless, its members will not act destructively or irresponsibly, because they are working at the request of their leader or superior (whether the relationship be formal or informal). It is not the terms of a contract (which would be signed on such an occasion) but personal sincerity towards one's leader or superior that requires the member to undertake the work of the committee.

Because of such arrangements, an organizing committee always consists of a relatively large number of members, among whom only a handful are really active or productive. Even among the active members, some would work willingly and contribute in great measure towards the business in hand, while others would not be given much to do, in that their abilities are not necessarily appropriate to the work (the processes of recommendation do not always produce those best suited). This Japanese practice entails the same individual holding possibly several additional posts, for in some of the committees he may be needed simply for the sake of his name, with his participation in the actual work of the committees being only slight or even non-existent. This situation appears most markedly in the case of a top man senior in years who is able to mobilize many men junior to him for different purposes. Such a senior person might well have collected so many honorary positions that he himself cannot readily remember them all. Indeed, some of the honorary positions he holds might well be quite unrelated to his specialization: this matters little, for what is required of him is his capacity to mobilize his juniors, rather than any special ability in a particular kind of work. Such positions contribute to a higher social prestige and, in turn, higher prestige invites more positions. An organizer should have a set of names of persons of high prestige who will not only collect members essential for the work but will also give the convention respectability and a sound standard. In view of such overlapping and the accumulation of positions, the picture of such organizations becomes very complicated. However, when they are viewed in terms of the ∧ shape structure to which the individual is primarily attached it becomes clear that the basic operation of the organizing principle derives from constant vertical personal links.

There has recently been a growth in criticism of the existence in political circles of *habatsu* (factions). Such criticism led to declarations by successive prime ministers, Ikeda and Satō, as well as other leading political figures, of their intention to break down the *habatsu* and, as a result, move in the direction of what they term 'modern' politics. But, in spite of such pious statements, there is as yet no evidence of a lessening or weakening of *habatsu* activities, whether among conservatives or socialists. This is not surprising, for if, even among those who claim to be 'modern intellectuals', the establishment of the personal relation based on contract is so difficult and has had so little currency, we could hardly expect success in an attempt by politicians to substitute it for the *habatsu*.

Should these ∧ form relationships be abolished, their place would be taken by another form of organization. In theory, only two alternatives are possible: the first is the adoption of a system based on horizontal relationships; but this would not necessarily be better than a system based on *oyabun–kobun* relationships, for it has much in common with nepotism and is open to monopolization by some particular group. In addition, such a system would not find favour with the Japanese without some fundamental change in the Japanese character.

The second alternative is to depend on 'contract' relationships – as, when Kennedy organized his Administration, he chose, on the basis of their abilities, men with whom he had no personal relationship – Rusk, the Republican MacNamara (in the Japanese vernacular this is called 'doing business with the enemy'). This method, however, presupposes the sense of 'contract', and it seems (to me at least) it is this possibility of contract that makes American and British politics incomparably superior to Japanese politics. By my analysis, the possibility just does not exist in Japan.

The development of the modern contract system in the West, and its failure in Japan, seems to me to be traceable not to any differences in degree of industrialization but rather to the existence and persistence of native values manifested ever since the feudal age in the relationship between lord and subject. Plurality of lords, permissible in the West, was refused all countenance in Japan: 'a man cannot serve two masters' it was said, and if the relationship continued from generation to generation so much the better. The nature of the relationship between lord and subject was also quite different. In the West the relationship involved an embryonic notion of the modern contract, while in Japan it meant a life-long commitment, embodying an ideology far divorced from any sense of contract. The difficulty of establishing contractual relations along western lines in a modern industrial enterprise in Japan has already been illustrated in the historical background of the life-employment system (see pp. 14–18 above). It would appear that management, while searching for methods of guaranteeing a constant labour supply, passed over the contract system as a means of holding on to labour (particularly skilled labour) and hit on the career employment system so aptly suited to the Japanese.

To sum up: for a variety of reasons it is difficult for a

Japanese to establish operational contractual personal relations. First, it is hard for a Japanese to differentiate his rôles (I shall discuss this point in detail in the next section) and, once a relationship is established, both parties tend to expect more from it than work itself, and so involve themselves emotionally: only through this involvement can they feel certain that the operation in question will be performed smoothly and effectively. Moreover, each party tends to monopolize his partner's loyalty, though it may be utterly unnecessary for the completion of the work. His emotional security seems the foremost requirement for a Japanese engaged in co-operative work. Second, in Japan it is very difficult to form a corporate group by inviting those best suited to the work in question; everyone is already more or less involved in a particular group – and the links and loyalties thus established will not easily be cut. If a man is invited to join a new group he may try his best, as a mother hen with her brood, to take along his whole entourage to the new group; or he may still hold loyally to his former group. These factors intimately affect the functioning of the new group. Because loyalty is emotional, it does not lend itself to division.

4. The undifferentiated rôle of the group member

In the foregoing section I have pointed out that the realms of leader and subordinate are not clearly marked, and that responsibility is diffused through the group as a whole. This applies not merely to the relationship between leader and subordinate but as well to all interpersonal relations within the group. The distinguishing characteristic of the operation of the group is seen to be the absence of clearly differentiated rôles for each according to his position. The formal organization of the group assigns to each member a certain prescribed rôle which he is to perform. However, in practice the informal organization of the group takes precedence, and such formally prescribed rôles are not always performed according to expectation. The actual rôle of an individual does not always or necessarily correspond to his rank or status. Rank functions to maintain the legitimate order in interpersonal relations, particularly when it is operating externally, but does not bind the member within the limits of an ascribed rôle. On the contrary, when the group is in action the rôles of individual members are readily adjustable to changing situations. Rank and rôle operate on different principles; the rigidity in the order of rank is offset by the resiliency in the individual's rôle in action.

In this system the individual has the advantage of great freedom of action. For the group there is advantage to be gained from the effective mobilzation of the group force by maximizing the potential ability of individual members. The following illustration will make this point clearer. Let us take a group consisting of three members, X, Y and Z, in which each member is assigned his rôle according to his respective position. When a rôle is clearly differentiated in terms of the ideology of the division of labour each member is expected to offer service consistent with his rôle, regardless of any variations of situation in which the group is involved. Now let us suppose that the group is faced with a situation in which the service of Y is in great demand. If the group is based on a clear differentiation of rôles the performance of the work may require, say, three days. But if the group is one in which the principle of differentiation of rôles is not strongly established the same amount of work may be achieved in one day because X and Z also take on the rôle of Y.

Thus the adaptability of the group in action is enhanced, but a system of this kind is adopted only by people who have little concern for the principle of the division of labour. It is obvious that in Japan the ideology of the division of labour is not well developed, and the Japanese in general hold fairly strong convictions that one man can do another's job whenever this be necessary. A Japanese is rarely satisfied in a job unless he is able to visualize the whole of the operation being undertaken by the group of which he is a member. He may also tend to overestimate the importance of individual rôles within his organization, for he tends easily to overstep the domain of his prescribed rôle. There is a well-known tendency for the

Japanese to undertake requests even when they fall outside his sphere of competence. This is the very antithesis of the convictions of the Hindus and their caste system.

Japanese practice is also in sharp contrast with western usage, and ideological differences in this regard can be observed regularly in daily life. Japanese (and I include myself among them) are often surprised in the West by the rejection of a small request by a person who sits next to one with whom they are supposed to deal, but who is busy or absent at the time. The Japanese reaction is that of puzzlement and an inability to appreciate why the official rejected such an easy and trifling request by saying it was not his job. If he had readily acceded to the request things would have gone more efficiently. Here Japanese find an unexpected rigidity in the West, although they are obliged to marvel at the westerner's ability to preserve such neat compartments and divisions of function.

The individual's freedom of action within a Japanese organization also allows him to give more or less than the prescribed amount of service. He can be very dedicated or very lazy; the choice is his. The system allows for differences of temperament and talent, for, since the individual's rôle is not defined explicitly and he is not expected to give a regular and specified amount of service, he can make his contribution more or less as he is inclined. The group thus maintains a potential labour force the magnitude of which it is difficult to measure in technical terms. Degrees of contribution from individual members may differ from person to person, and degrees of contribution from any one individual may vary according to personal condition or temperament at any given time. But whereas a system based on the ideology of the division of labour entails impersonalization, this system retains, or even encourages, personal elements: the social control and the expectation of an individual's participation is less rigorous than in a system based on a division of labour, where one must always be ready to perform one's rôle in a consistent manner. According to the Japanese system, work is always assigned to a group, for example, to a section of an organization, and performed in the name of the group, not by a particular individual. In an actual operation the head of the group distributes a share of the work to individuals according to the given 'situation' of group members. This system entails a somewhat unfair distribution of the work, since an able member tends to carry a greater amount than a less able members.

Normally, in any such group there will be a very busy member and at the same time a man with little work to do, even though the two may receive the same amount of payment. The reward given to the man who offers greater service is not measured in economic terms, but instead takes a social form. He may be regarded as of great capability and receive warm appreciation from his fellow-members, particularly from the leader; he enjoys the feeling of being a man of importance, and his voice in the group may increase accordingly, whereas a lazy man who contributes less remains a somewhat marginal figure in the group.

The limits of individual freedom of action are fixed in such a way as to ensure that the activity of the individual will not breach group limits. Freedom is allowed only in directions allowed for in group decisions. Action should be always for the group, not calculated in terms of the individual. Whatever the amount of one's contribution may be, it will not lead to any change in the order of rank. Gains from individual contributions are thus shared by the whole group. Loyalty towards the group forms the basis on which individual activity is carried out. It is this moral facet which allows a man who contributes little to remain in the group, comfortably keeping his status so long as he remains loyal and does not run counter to group activity.

Whether an individual contribution is over or under par is largely dependent on the emotional harmony of the group, for which the leader is mainly responsible. It is for this reason that in Japan every manager attaches a high degree of importance to the relationships among his employees. There are also to be found here grounds for the defence of the seniority system against the merit system. The seniority system is criticized as entailing loss of productivity in the case of a capable individual because it prohibits promotion of an able young man to a higher post where his ability could be properly used, and thus contains latent frustration for a capable young man. This criticism, however, presupposes that the individual position corresponds to a defined rôle. Against this, it can be argued in favour of the seniority system that it does allow utilization of the ability of the young man, and at a lower cost in fact, for this is quite possible when rôles are not strictly defined. The net result of both systems seems to be rather evenly balanced. However, the Japanese seniority system involves variable and unpredictable elements which make it difficult to attain consistency and to establish standards of achievement.

When such a wide range of action is open to him much depends on the individual's incentive. This system can compete with the merit system only if the individual member's contribution reaches above par. This is well established in the statement of a Japanese manager.

Employer and employee in my company are bound by fate. When a set of persons comes together to work, the result is not always to be stated in simple mathematical terms as one plus one makes two. If two persons join forces, they may produce as much as three or five times as much as a single individual, or, if they fail to get on good terms, the result may be zero. If there are troubles among employees, their employer is ill-qualified as a manager. The company with good human relations will have incentives and will succeed in its business.

This view is shared by almost all Japanese managers. However, there remains the problem of how this system can accommodate itself to automation and high technical specialization.

This accommodation is indeed the crucial point facing managers today. In the course of the fantastic economic development of post-war Japan, along with the introduction of highly improved technical equipment, modern management (as developed particularly in the United States) has become the great concern of Japanese managers and sociologists specializing in management. Hundreds of books and thousands of magazine and journal essays have been devoted to discussing the issue of the introduction of American-style management. The major arguments concern the advisability of the change from the seniority system to the merit system. In the main, managers seem still to be retaining faith in the seniority system, while scholars and critics urge more and more insistently a change to the merit system. Managers say they cannot risk their companies; it is for them a matter of life and death, while for the scholars it is simply a matter of academic debate.

This problem is intimately linked with an issue most interesting from a anthropological point of view. The formal organization and the productive system of a large factory or business firm in Japan are of the same pattern as those in the United States. However, the informal organization is profoundly different, so different that it is difficult to imagine a change in the informal structure which has been the driving force of Japan's industrial development. A shift from the seniority to the merit system would involve not a partial or technical change in payment or promotion methods but a drastic reformation of the structure itself, beginning with the basic orientation of native values. The merit system could be applied only in a very limited and specific way, as, for example, in a section of a large company comprising engineers with highly specialized qualifications or in a comparatively new and small private firm and so on; it is difficult to envisage it being applied generally in the case of a large institutional organization. It is important here to remember that the informal structure within the factory or firm is closely linked with and derived from the overall social organization of the country. A major change will inevitably invite confusion and conflict, and many managers hold the view that the result of a reform might be an evil far more difficult to face than the existing disease.

The traditional system in group operation in Japan is based on the conviction that the energy produced by the group as a whole brings the most effective results; the net contribution of each individual tends to be disregarded. The system thought of as backward and feudalistic by many Japanese progressive intellectuals, particularly in comparison with the American system, is now, interestingly enough, much more in line with the orientation taking place even in the United States, which puts a growing empahasis on 'organizational power' or 'teamwork'. Here the rôle of the individual tends to be less marked, and success is attributed to effective organization or teamwork. Though the Japanese version of group organization may differ in internal structure from that of the West, in both cases the form coincides. In this sense it would not be proper to regard the Japanese system as simply backward; on the contrary, given the conditions of the modern world, it may be said to be very efficient, and may, in fact, be one of the reasons why Japanese industry has been successful in developing to a point where it is well able to compete with the advanced countries of the West.

3   The Overall Structure
of the Society

The overall picture of society resulting from such inter-personal (and inter-group) relations is not that of horizontal stratification by class or caste but of vertical stratification by institution or group of institutions. The construction of social groups based on vertical organization stresses the unitary aspect and brings about numerous vertical schisms within the society. Even if social classes like those in Europe can be detected in Japan, and even if something vaguely resembling those classes that are illustrated in the textbooks of western sociology can also be found in Japan, the point is that in actual society this stratification is unlikely to function and that it does not really reflect the social structure. In Japanese society it is really not a matter of workers struggling against capitalists or managers but of Company A ranged against Company B. The protagonists do not stand in vertical relationship to each other but instead rub elbows from parallel positions. The organization of unions in Japan, their ideals and the peculiarities to be seen in the union movement cannot be understood without this kind of analysis. The antagonism and wrangling between management and labour in Japan is unquestionably a 'household' problem, and though their basic divergence is the same as it is the world over, the reason it cannot develop in Japan into a problem intimately and powerfully affecting society as a whole is to be found in the group structure and the nature of total Japanese society.

Because competition takes place between parallel groups of the same kind, the enemy is always to be found among those in the same category. (In other societies such groups could be linked by co-operative ties which would represent a totally opposite kind of strength in relations.) To illustrate this, competition arises among the various steel companies, or among import–export firms. Among schools it is just the same; university against university, high school against high school. In rural areas competition develops among neighbouring villages and also among households within a village; in religious communities, among older Buddhist sects and among newly established religious groups. In the bureaucracy it may be that the Home Ministry wrangles with the Foreign Office.

If this competition is expressed very pragmatically the prize in the race is the rating. A common Japanese reaction may well take the form, 'Their rating is higher than ours, so ...' Among governmental organizations the ranking is known in an informal way, though in a manner sufficiently overt for those closely concerned. The Finance Ministry stands out at the top, and the Education Ministry, for example, is placed considerably lower. Generally, earlier entrants (those having a longer history) have the higher ratings, but the fact that rating can be changed through the acquisition of additional political and economic power and influence is a primary factor in whipping up the race.

This rating protocol is exemplified in its traditional form by the ranking of households in a village community. There have been numerous studies of hierarchy in village politics by rural sociologists in Japan; indeed, the villagers' sharp awareness of it compares with the caste-consciousness in a Hindu village. The ranking hierarchy was normally determined by the relative length of establishment of each household in the village. Thus the older tended to be ranked higher, but wealth was an additional factor (though never the primary one) in determining rating. Along with this fairly stable ranking, there was a custom by which every village community made an annual roster of its households, called *kotōhyō*, in which all households of the village were listed in order from top to bottom, with an internal grading into several classes, according to actual wealth and income, and efficiency in handling money. This evaluation was made by the members of the village council through close observation of the villagers' daily lives.* Hence the rating order normally differed from the official listings of income for taxation purposes made by public offices. This record was not designed merely to give prestige to those listed higher; it also served the welfare of the community, for those households accorded higher rank were assessed larger shares of the costs of communal activities. If the village economy was stable both social and economic rankings would be fairly closely matched.

Such rankings, which were of great weight in the establishment of the social order, stimulated competition among households with relatively similar standing. Aged farmers can still recall today stories and anecdotes relating to such competition. For example, they would try their best to get up earlier than their neighbours, for it was thought that the actual number of work hours paralleled the volume of production. So, to forestall neighbours from being up as early as themselves, they would open their sliding doors very quietly, and carry any noisy farming tools, such as rollers, so as to avoid making any sound when they passed their neighbours' houses. The degree reached by such competition even prompted inhumane excesses. I was told by one old woman in a comparatively poor village that it was the greatest pleasure of her life when her neighbour's store building caught fire.

Competition over rating between households, once the great concern of tradition-bound villages, is in its modern variant of great concern to contemporary urban society. Rating of high schools, for example, closely parallels the rating of the traditional households. It is true that older and well-established schools are placed higher, but there are some changes occasioned by the yearly records showing numbers of students successful in the entrance examinations for the highest-ranked universities. An executive of a big steel company stated openly that his company's goal is to get ahead of Yawata Steel, which

* This *kotōhyō* was not intended for disclosure to outsiders and, so far as I know, there have been no specific studies ever made of it, in spite of its widespread usage and its tradition going back to the Tokugawa period.

stands highest among steel companies in Japan. Such competition among enterprises certainly contributes to economic development by concentrating the energies of individual enterprises, and competition is both an important element in toughening the intra-group unity towards which Japanese managers are always aiming and a powerful factor in encouraging independence and isolation (as was noted in Chapter Two).

However, at the same time such headlong competition entails an unavoidable and unwarranted waste of energy. In foreign trade the dog-eat-dog spectacle of many companies offering the same product to the same buyers is well known. In Japan someone has only to say, 'I think cabbages are good', for the farmers all to yell, 'Me too, me too', and everyone plants cabbages; in the following year cabbages flood the market and rot in the fields. One or two publishers succeed with paperbacks and every company starts to put out the same series, with the same old authors saying the same old things. One of the most reputable publishers came to me one day asking for ideas for his company's new line of paperback books. I asked why they, too, should have added the same supplementary line as the others. His reply was, 'You can't help it, you know, it brings in the money. There is no other publisher as big as ourselves who has not started it.' And I was told further that the publishing houses are fostering the recent trend for books to be mass-produced commodities which everybody can buy, throw away after use and then be supplied at once with new ones. It seems too, that authors have become mere employees in the pay of editors of publishing companies. Otherwise, a publishing house runs the risk of failing to qualify to be classed as 'modern'.

This prodigality appears to be one of the aspects of modern progress in Japan. Yet the companies maintain their traditional practice of achievement through competition, without giving any consideration to possible diversification. They seem not to be satisfied unless they are all doing the same thing. They do it because they mustn't lose the race, they can't miss the bus. Yet even though Japan is no doubt better off than underdeveloped countries, with a tradition of absolute division of labour as incisive as India's, there must yet be some way to cut down on such inexcusable waste of the nation's resources.

The competitive race which results in the apparent independence and isolation of each institution, at the same time entails the establishment of a hierarchical order among similar institutions; so, in spite of mutual hostility, they form together one social world in which they are deeply enmeshed. In fact, in reality they are not entirely disconnected; rather, a number of similar institutions is pulled together, even though by negative elements. They fall into groups such as heavy industrial enterprises, service enterprises, governmental organizations, publishers, universities, etc. Within each world the concern of one institution with all the others engaged in similar activity is so deep that it is astonishing how closely they are informed, though each will try its best to conceal its affairs from the rest.* If asked, anyone involved in such a situation would be in a position at once to outline the hierarchy in his field, for the ranking order of the several institutions is generally acknowledged. Even outside the group, there is a fairly clear picture of the ranking order.

Indeed, this ranking hierarchy is to be found in every field; once an order is established, it will continue over a considerable period of time in spite of ups and downs in actual circumstances. This is, in the main, because one of the chief criteria of the rating is the relative length of the history of an institution; one with a longer history which has maintained a fairly high rank normally holds a number of advantages in its activities over those rated beneath it. Once the status of an institution is recognized as of top rank, this status is maintained even when its activities are inferior to those ranked lower; time, backed by bald facts, is required before change can occur. For example, a company ranked at the top in Japanase estimation may not necessarily be one with the best showing in recent years as far

* It is said that a concern will employ a number of 'industrial spies' to get secret information regarding other successful enterprises.

as profits go, but the name of the company and its products have been widely known over a long period.

Top-ranking institutions are called *ichi-ryū* (first rate), a very favourite term of the Japanese which carries great sociological significance. *Ichi-ryū gaisha* means the top-ranking company; *ichi-ryū-kō* is the top-ranking school; such institutions carry the highest prestige as being at the apex of the hierarchy in a given field. *Ichi-ryū* normally includes more than one institution, though there is a ranking order among those classed as *ichi-ryū*, and there is only one at the very top. Organizations in a given field classed as *ichi-ryū* normally stand close to each other, with a wide gap between this category and those classed as *ni-ryū* (second rate). However, *ni-ryū* and *san-ryū* (third rate) do not represent independent categories but rather those not included within the *ichi-ryū* group. *Ichi-ryū* means 'above all' or 'ideal'. The ranking of individual institutions within the *ni-ryū* and *san-ryū* category is not always clear; one of the clues to the comparative ranking is to be found in the amount each institution will donate to a public fund; if A, the top company in a given field, gives x pounds the rest in that field will donate in accordance with their ranking, B giving a third of x, C a tenth of x and so on. In just the same way, in the case of a public fund for a village shrine festival, each household in the village will contribute in accordance with calculations based on the *kotōhyō*, the acknowledged social and economic ranking of all the households in a village community.

Those classified as *ni-ryū* and *san-ryū* are in constant competition with each other and always striving for promotion to *ichi-ryū* status. This ever-present consciousness of ranking contributes to the encouragement of competition among peers. In fact, it does seem that this social impetus is even more keenly felt and appreciated than the desire to show better profits: it is the former, rather, which prompts expansion and a higher investment rate, or the construction of attractive modern offices and factories. In this sense, Japanese values are orientated rather to sociological than economic goals. This conclusion also emerges from a consideration of the social psychology of the individual.

The ranking order among institutions is likewise of immediate concern to individuals, in that individual status and prestige go according to this ranking as well as according to the individual's rank within each institution. Even typists and drivers take a pride in belonging to a company with a high ranking, for they are able to feel superior to typists and drivers employed by lesser-ranked companies, even though they receive the same pay.

The Japanese are not so much concerned with social background as with institutional affiliation. Since the hierarchy of each field is so clearly perceived and widely known, and since the hierarchy within individual institutions also extends beyond the institution, these credentials taken together offer a fairly distinct picture into which an individual can be fitted. Among directors of companies, ranks will accord with the ranks of their respective companies; a departmental head of a large, highly rated company would be located in a rank comparable with that of a director of a smaller company; a professor in a minor university would be equated with a lecturer or assistant professor of a high-ranked university and so on. In this respect the order of rank underlying the structure of Japanese society serves a function similar to a classification by caste or class, by which the individual is located. This, I think, is the reason why the Japanese care so little about class differences. They are more interested in their relative rank, and so attention is focused upon the self and those in the immediate surroundings. The Japanese in general are virtually incapable of seeing society in terms of strata within which one may locate oneself, yet they will employ delicately graded criteria to distinguish the most minor relative differences between themselves and others.

The building of a hierarchy based on the ranking order of institutions is further complicated by the tendency for a set of institutions to be organized in the manner of the formula Λ, in just the same way as individuals form a group. It is usual, for example, for a large business firm or industrial plant to attach to itself a considerable number of affiliated and subordinate companies, many of which are called its 'child-companies'. The nature and degree of the relationships between 'parent-company' and 'child-company' vary considerably. A 'child-company' may be created by separating a part of the original company, or by investing a part of the capital of the latter; or an independent smaller company may establish a parent and child relationship with a large one. Personnel and finance may be transferred from the one to the other. However, some child-companies have a considerable degree of independence from the parent company and an autonomy not to be found in the case of, for example, an American subsidiary company. Indeed, there are examples of a child-company developing and becoming so successful as to reach a status comparable with that of its parent company. On the other hand, a child-company may be closely tied to the parent-company, forming one distinct hierarchical organization together with other companies affiliated to them at various levels. It is usual for this hierarchical organization to be centred on a large company with more than,

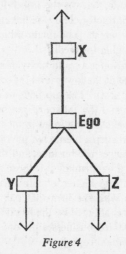

Figure 4

say, 10,000 employees, while, at the lowest level, there may be a very small enterprise consisting of the members of a single family.

The entire system is rather like a segmentary system, in terms of social anthropology. However, it is not the recognition of the entire system that is important for the various individual enterprises which constitute such a group; what is important is the linkage between the immediate two: one (X) from which information and orders come to *ego* (institution), and the other (Y or Z) to which *ego* sends information and orders (see Figure 4). The actual number of the latter may well be more than two, but the relationship with each is established and exists independently. Similarly, there may be more than one X, but there is invariably a particular X which is more closely involved and takes precedence over the others.

This segmentary system, therefore, is not the core of group formation; rather, it results from the accumulation or the successive extension of a single linkage between two institutions. The linkage between two particular institutions is very important: for the one on the lower level it is the main route for business orders, while that on the upper level links thus with an important subcontractor. Thus the linkage contains constant mutual economic interests. The relationship creates credit; the longer it lasts, the higher the credit.

Since an organization is a multiplicity of such relationships, it may often occur that at the lower level the source of information or business is not known. The top pays little attention to links at the lowest level, and the sphere of responsibility extends no further than to those standing in an immediate relation to *ego*. It is obvious that, in such a hierarchy, the higher the location of an enterprise, the larger the business and therefore the less the risk. In the case of a bankruptcy it is those at the bottom of the scale who suffer; those higher remain unaffected and merely terminate relations with the firm that has gone bankrupt and those at a lower level affected by the bankruptcy. In the case of two immediately related businesses the one ranked higher may offer to stave off the bankruptcy.

Clusters of this kind, which exist in all business sectors in Japan, are to be seen at their most pronounced in such fields as automobile production and the building industry. Toyota Motor Corporation, one of the largest automobile enterprises in Japan, is a convenient and telling illustration. Centred on Toyota Motor Corporation are twelve companies known as the Toyota Group. These companies are closely linked with Toyota Motor Corporation through activities or business such as sales, exports, production of parts and supply of materials. They have a direct relationship to the central Toyota Motor Corporation (the Japanese term, *chokkei kigyō*, means enterprises in direct line). Top executives are often transferred between these companies within the Toyota Group; members of the Toyota family – brothers, sons, grandsons, nephews and sons-in-law – take the top positions, although the posts of president and director are not invariably the exclusive preserve of family members (see pp. 113–14). Capital can also be passed readily and swiftly between these directly linked companies in case of emergency.

In addition to this group of directly linked companies there are roughly a further two hundred plants and factories aligned under Toyota Motor Corporation, on the basis of a linear relationship (the Japanese term is *keiretsu*). Most of these are specialist parts producers, although there are many variations in the nature of the relationship with Toyota Motor Corporation and in the scale of operations undertaken for the parent company. Some are linked to the latter through capital investment, while others may be more independent enterprises. K Factory, for example, employs fifty men, in a plant which occupies 330 square metres, in the production of various types of spring. The whole of K Factory's production goes exclusively to C Company, from which it is again passed on to C's parent company, Toyota Motor Corporation, and other major automobile assemblers. Below K Company there is a further series of child-companies working for K, the great bulk of which are of cottage-industry standard, employing no more than the head of the household and members of his family.

It is very interesting to note that these relationships – called parent–child (*oyako*) by the Japanese – between modern industrial enterprises are identical in structure with those between traditional agricultural households on a landowner-and-tenant basis in rural Japan.*

It seems, then, that an organizational principle in terms of parent–child relationships constitutes the basic scheme of Japanese organization. This principle is to be found in almost every kind of institution in Japan: a top-ranking university, for example, attaches to itself a number of smaller and local universities and colleges, to which it supplies graduates as teaching staff. Religious communities also offer a typical example of this segmentary system; temples (in Buddhism) and shrines (in Shintō) are organized in accordance with this kind of hierarchical system, each sect maintaining its own rating system. The hierarchical organization of religious institutions involves more administrative functions than those of industrial institutions, since, except for a few original sects, most religious institutions originated from a separation movement from an older order. The various Buddhist sects have manifested this organizational pattern throughout Japan's history. Each sect has a main (original) temple or monastery which stands at the apex of the organization and controls other branch or subordinate temples and monasteries. Each subordinate branch has a place within the organization determined by the date and method of its establishment within the ∧ hierarchy. The sect thus develops a highly centralized autonomy. (It is very interesting to compare this with monastic organizations in Tibet, Thailand, Burma and so on, where no elaborate hierarchical organization such as that in Japan has ever developed.) In Japan the cluster grouping is so powerful that Buddhist priests of different sects hardly meet together, and find it quite impossible to attend services together. Laymen, too, are clearly classified by temple: members of a particular household are always affiliated to a particular temple, never two or more. It would be out of the question to summon a priest of a different sect or to make a donation to a temple

* For these, known as *dōzoku* or *oyako-kankei*, see Nakane, *Kinship and Economic Organization in Rural Japan*, London, 1967, pp. 82–132.

other than one's own, except in the case of an old-established and wealthy aristocratic household, which used to contribute to several temples.

The same basic pattern is evident in the organization of the new religious groups, such as Tenrikyō and Sōka-gakkai, which have been particularly successful in the period after the second world war. Tenrikyō began much earlier than Sōka-gakkai and had already developed successfully before the war. In its system the main (original) church stands at the apex and dominates a number of branch churches (which are classified in terms of major and minor) scattered throughout Japan and among large Japanese communities abroad, such as in Hawaii and in Brazil. To these churches (including the main) numerous individual churches are attached, some of them little larger in scale than a private household. Individual members in one way or other affiliated to one of these churches thus together form the single large community of Tenrikyō. The church affiliation of an individual derives from the church of the person through whom he was converted to Tenrikyō. Hence the system of the organization cuts across local community boundaries. For example, a major branch church may be known by the name of the prefecture in which it is established, but its members are not necessarily resident in the prefecture. At a later stage in its development, after membership had greatly increased so that a large number was to be found in the same locality, a new local grouping system was introduced, which cut across these vertical lines. The horizontal grouping, however, is only of a complementary nature, and the main arteries of the organization remain in the vertical lines.

Besides its links with larger and smaller institutions of its own kind, each institution has constant dealings with an array of differing institutions, for example, those supplying necessary services; together, they form still another functional group. A bank, an insurance company, an industrial plant, an export–import firm, a shipping company and other numerous related operations might form one group. (These were indeed the component elements of a *Zaibatsu*. *Zaibatsu* monopoly was not directed to a particular interest, but covered a wide range of interests in industry.* Though the *Zaibatsu* were disbanded under the policy of the American occupation, the principle of their organization survived below the surface.)

Within the group, duties and obligations are so rigorous that there is very little opportunity for the entry of others. As an example, there is a story of a famous French designer who was invited to show his collection by one of the largest department stores in Tokyo and required a particular material for some of his designs. Unfortunately, this material was not made by the textile firms supplying this particular department store, so he asked that the store should get the material from another textile company. However, he finally had to give up hope in the face of strong resistance shown by the department store on the grounds that the firm which made the particular material did not have established dealings with the store.

The widely observed Japanese ethic is that, once firmly established, a relationship should be maintained even despite economic loss. Such loss, however, may be offset in the long run, since the rigid relationship develops a high credit relationship benefiting mutual interests. The degree of independence of a single institution in Japan is minimal, that of a group extremely high. Each group is known informally as 'of the line of A' or 'descended from A', and the word *kei*, signifying descent or genealogical relationship, symbolizes the Japanese social system.

An examination of the inter-institutional relations in any group reveals the operation of the same structural mechanism as exists in the single institution: immobility, both within and between groups. For this reason, a group, on whatever level, is organized vertically and keeps its solidarity and exclusiveness. For the same reason, any element built into the body of the group is virtually unexchangeable. Thus the one-to-one, single-

*These comprised mining, metals, mechanical engineering, electrical apparatus and machinery, textiles, paper, cement, glass, chemicals, shipbuilding, shipping, foreign and domestic trade, banking and insurance. (See G. C. Allen, *A Short Economic History of Modern Japan*, New York, 1963, p. 134.)

bond affiliation, solidly fixed, contributes to the maintenance of order in the overall structure of society. It is not a simple matter of 'loyalty', for the structure of the group is significant. A society having this type of social organization does not spontaneously pool its resources from which every group can take supplies whenever needed. In this system of organization, therefore, a group tends to develop self-sufficiency so that it can function by itself: otherwise, it would not survive.

The need for self-sufficiency and the still greater need to compete successfully breed another distinguishing characteristic of institutions, a uniformity of pattern among those with similar activities and interests. The activities and the range of interests of each *Zaibatsu* unit and of the larger grouped enterprises today have striking similarities. Such similarity of pattern derives from the competitive urge driving every institution or group of institutions to imitate the pattern of the similar institution which stands right at the top of the hierarchy: rivals and competitors seek for the source of the success of the institution at the top in its operational pattern. Hence a 'standard pattern' always tends to appear in every field of activity.

The outstanding characteristic of the standard pattern is that it should cover a wide range of interests and include many varying items or services, thus completing a 'one-set' service that in itself can fulfil all the needs of a customer. Japan's newspapers afford an appropriate example of this 'one-set' service. For each of the three largest daily newspapers in Japan circulation ranges around 5,000,000 copies. Each has morning and evening issues. The coverage of the contents and the layout are surprisingly similar. Besides the usual contents of a daily newspaper, such as foreign and local news, sports news, women's columns and advertisements, each contains essays by scholars, critics, artists and writers on various subjects, including literary reviews; each carries one comic and one or two popular fiction serials which usually run for several months. These papers are meant to attract everyone from leading intellectual to worker. Their style, the arrangement of columns and the contents are so very similar among the three as to suggest that there could be no alternative format for a newspaper. The differences are so minor that there is hardly any need to subscribe to more than one, unless to have every detail of news or to enjoy a very slight variation in manner of reporting. Naturally, the three compete ferociously for top place in the hierarchy.

The 'one-set' pattern is also evident in educational institutions. The new universities established since the war – and there are now over eight hundred universities and colleges – follow the pattern of the old-established top-ranking institutions. They cover all fields – the natural sciences, the technologies, the humanities and the social sciences – and thus fail to develop a special strength in a particular field. The result is that the top-ranking universities, with their greater funds and higher prestige, monopolize every field: the mobility of both teachers and students between institutions is restricted. These circumstances lead to an openly and generally acknowledged ranking of the universities, with those rated at the top able to monopolize every academic field, and with graduates assessed according to the ranking of their university. This, of course, has a direct bearing on the chances of employment of a graduate, and in fact, top-ranking enterprises tend to recruit only from graduates of the top universities: in some cases graduates of universities of lower standing are not even given the chance to submit an application to such enterprises. Thus the status of enterprises and universities corresponds quite closely, and there are many instances of, as it were, a direct route from particular university to particular enterprise.

Development of this standard pattern on the 'one-set' principle is evident also in minor fields. A striking example is the lunch prepared by a local station in Japan and sold at every railway restaurant. A small box luncheon called *makunouchi* contains every single item of cooked food considered neecssary or representative of Japanese taste: small pieces of fish and beef, baked or fried, seasoned with soy sauce; omelettes; well-cooked seaweed and vegetables, cucumber or radish pickles; and a sliced piece of an apple or an orange. These occupy a half or a third of the box space, and the rest is filled with cooked white rice. In any station throughout Japan this box lunch is available, and one can be almost certain to predict its exact contents before one opens the box. The difference is to be found in the quality of the materials and the cooking; form and contents are identical.

Like the Japanese lunch box, every group in Japan tends to include an almost identical variety or selection of elements so that it does not require the services of other groups. The lack of interdependence between groups – division of labour in a sociological sense – is also evident in the composition of a traditional village (this again, in marked contrast with the Hindu caste village). In the pre-modern Japanese village hardly any household specialized in any occupation other than agriculture, the only exceptions being the blacksmith, for instance, the general store and the local priest. Every peasant household lived by its own agricultural produce and wove its own clothes; even funerals were conducted by neighbours in co-operation, the priest being the only specialist engaged. A village rarely needed the services of other villages or men engaged in occupations other than farming.

This is completely the opposite of the caste ideology, in which division of labour and the interdependence of groups are the basic principles of social organization. In a caste society groups are formed of homogeneous elements, while in Japan they consist of heterogeneous elements. It follows that in the caste society each group possesses some unique quality, the function of which cannot be filled by any other group. Through the meshing of these unique group functions society can spontaneously organize itself into one entity. In such a society each group must have positive relations with other groups possessing different rôles and activities respectively. Where groups are homogeneous, there is need of mutual services between groups. This mechanism serves to organize a number of heterogeneous groups into a large social body. By contrast, a Japanese group, the internal composition of which is heterogeneous, has a character homogeneous with that of many other groups. Hence there is no necessity for positive relations with other groups; instead, relations tend to be hostile or competitive. In Japan, however large a field or segment of the population may be served by a 'one-set' group, its limits are automatic because of the nature of its function. Thus the entire society is a sort of aggregation of numerous independent competing groups which of themselves can make no links with each other: they lack a sociological framework on which to build up a complete and integrated society.

These characteristics of Japanese society assist the development of the state political organization. Competing clusters, in view of the difficulty of reaching agreement or consensus between clusters, have a diminshed authority in dealings with the state administration. Competition and hostile relations between the civil powers facilitate the acceptance of state power and, in that a group is organized vertically, once the state's administrative authority is accepted, it can be transmitted without obstruction down the vertical line of a group's internal organization. In this way the administrative web is woven more thoroughly into Japanese society than perhaps any other in the world.

In fact, in the Tokugawa period the effectiveness of the all-inclusive web of regulations emanating from the Shogunate and the feudal territories, reaching every village and household even up in the remote hill areas, was not simply a reflection of the power of the Shogunate; it should be looked on as issuing in large part from the nature of the structure of social groups. China and India, for example, in the same period provided striking contrasts; they had a strong horizontal social organization, and their central administration, hampered by the deep relationships constructed on horizontal bases (such as the network of patrilineal clan organizations, the landlord associations, guilds and castes), could influence no more than the upper strata of society, being quite unable to extend the basis of its authority throughout the whole population.

The development of the highly efficient and complex Japanese administrative network, its influence seeping through every section of society, serves all the more successfully to further the effectiveness of the central authority, and by the same token the pre-eminence of authority implants in the Japanese a ready submissiveness, alongside fear and hostility. They are afraid to offer open opposition to authority and instead commit themselves to it, while quietly admonishing one another to 'wrap yourself up in something long' or 'stand in the shadow of a big tree'. Obedience in Japan takes the form of total submission. Any criticism of or opposition to authority tends to be seen as heroism (and some of the leading intellectuals are always inclined to take the side of the visionary hero who seldom succeeds in attaining his goal). And, interestingly enough, such deeds are today labelled as democratic action. Often it is merely opposition for opposition's sake; it is nearer in essence to emotional contradiction than to the rational resistance from which further reasonable development might be expected.

Whatever its psychological or emotional effects, this penetrating power of the central administration, the roots of which were already well established in the Tokugawa period, was an essential basis for the rapid modernization which has taken place since the Meiji period. The bureaucratic system of this central administration has an organizational pattern in common with the Japanese native social structure – the vertical organizational principle of $\land$. The inception of the modern bureaucratic system in Japan did develop with the aid of the application of western patterns, but there was already an effective root in Japanese soil long before the advent of western influence, and it was by grafting to this living, native root that modern bureaucracy grew. It is evident through her history that if there is any strong and successful configuration in Japan it is always built on the same vertical lines that characterize the pattern of Japan's centralized administration.

4   Characteristics and Value Orientation of Japanese Man

1. From school to employment

The preceding chapters have offered an analysis of the structure of Japanese society. Now the focus of the discussion is turned to the individual who copes with the system, as a means of examining the present-day characteristics and value orientation of the Japanese.

The society in which class distinction is least developed offers man more opportunities for free competition on the road to success than class or caste societies. In general, in Japan a man's personal ability and actual achievements count for much more than family background. Whether an individual was born into a reputable or rich family or into a poor peasant family matters little after he has once gained admission to a successful group or has been given the chance of being linked with a successful or promising man. A man is classified primarily according to the group to which he belongs (or the individual to whom he is attached); assessment is in terms of his current activities, rather than the background of his birth. After admission to the group, provided that his ability and achievements are not below standard, it is almost certain he will be able to climb the vertical ladder of the internal hierarchy. Certainly, as he goes higher in the hierarchy he will face more intense competition with his colleagues, but the range of success and failure in such a limited field is not wide, however intense both his own and his peers' feelings within the group. Hence the decisive factor in success is the opportunity for entry to a particular group.

Since a group is based on a rigid hierarchical order, the individual is allowed to enter only at the bottom of the hierarchy; entry at any other point would disrupt the order and the links between existing members. In this system it is more advantageous for a man to remain in the same group than to move from one group to another. To stay in the same group is to climb the ladder in the course of time, since the group recruits new members who are placed beneath him, while older members above him fall out either through retirement or death; thus, in due time, he can accumulate a kind of social capital by remaining in the same group. This social capital, of course, cannot be transferred with him if he moves to another group.

It happens occasionally in the industrial field that a distinguished and highly qualified individual is invited to join another institution with the offer of a much higher salary. However, having climbed the ladder to be, say, section head, such an individual is normally reluctant to accept an offer, even if it amounts to twice or three times his existing salary. He would carefully calculate the economic gain against the loss of accumulated social capital: the company by which he is employed has prestige and pays him, at his rank, a salary no lower than is standard in Japan, though it is in no way appropriate to his ability and effort; the company has promised successive promotion so long as he stays with the company (and even without a contractual statement to this effect, he has faith in this promise). On the other hand, the company which has made the offer of a higher salary on the strength of his merit may not be able to guarantee similar promotion prospects – or at least he is unable to expect such promotion, in that he has not put in a long term of service. He thinks ahead to the point where his ability begins to wane; if he stays with his present company his future is assured and he will be promoted to a higher administrative office even after his talents and his usefulness begin to decline. Again, the change of companies would mean the loss of his colleagues and friends, and would put him into quite unfamiliar surroundings, where he would not be at all sure about personal relations – this is a vital consideration for a Japanese, as will be discussed in the next section. These considerations, then, of security and prestige, sufficiently outweigh the attraction of a much higher income and lead him in the end to decline the offer. He is familiar enough with the long series of tragic stories of those who changed jobs in the middle stages of their careers.

There are indeed many well-told stories in Japan of the new-comer, at an advanced stage in his career, making heavy weather in his new environment, even if he occupies a comparatively high post and obviously contributes a great deal to his new company. A very able middle-aged man has recently described his experiences in the following terms:

You know, it is not something to be explained logically. There were all sorts of disagreeable statements about me; it was not done in the context of formal business procedure but rather in the informal circumstances and networks in which I was unable to participate. It was, in fact, just like an old mother-in-law in a tradi-tional Japanese household getting at her young daughter-in-law over the salting of the pickled vegetables. She can never get it right, in the mother-in-law's eyes; either there's too much, so she's wasting salt, or there's too little so she has no idea how things should taste. So whatever I did invited criticism and complaint. There was never anything factual or any tangible reason. Rather it all came from spite – from their feeling that here was a new man who hadn't worked in the company from the start as they had done. In a situa-tion like this, a man can achieve his potential only when his boss is powerful enough to protect him against his colleagues. And when his boss retires, or if he should happen to leave, he would find him-self in a quite intolerable situation.

This case is by no means an exception. One executive, after ten years in one company, moved to another. Although he served his new company for twenty years and rose to be the manager of its London office, he was never fully accepted. (Perhaps it should be made clear that change of employment after retirement is not a part of the discussion at this point.)

Not only is it difficult to change one's job and adjust to new circumstances; it is also very hard to return to one's previous job after an interval of some years. Once a man leaves his job, his post is occupied immediately by the next in line to him, and it will be most difficult to find a vacancy for him when he expresses a wish to return. This is why it is very hard to find a man to take a post in an international organization such as UNESCO or ECAFE. Although one can find able men who are interested in such positions, they would not be prepared to take the risk, in that they know that, once a short-term contract is completed, they would not be assured of finding a job back in Japan that is as good as or better than the position they would leave. In the meanwhile, they would forfeit certain promotion, the right of him who stays. Japan's domestic system thus inhibits movement to international organizations; it also deters the really competent from participation in a new independent project, even if the term is limited. Such new projects are therefore put in the hands of those already firmly established or are given to those who have retired. As may be guessed from the composition of its personnel, the efficiency of such an enterprise is low in comparison with that of an established institution with regular, long-term personnel.

The difficulties placed in the way of changing employment in Japan lead to the practice of holding a plurality of posts simultaneously. This may well contribute to an increase in the prestige of the individual, but it does not increase efficiency. It is often observed, for instance, that a Japanese company carries more personnel than the work warrants; and, in the case of a joint project, organizers will strive to get well-known personalities of high status associated as members of the committee, to ensure a wider social recognition and higher esteem, even though these personalities are far too involved elsewhere to participate in the actual activities of the project. The prohibition on mobility in the Japanese system promotes inefficiency.

It has often been claimed recently that promotion by merit rather than seniority, on the American and western patterns, is becoming more attractive in Japan and, indeed, that modern management is changing to this practice. In fact, however, there has been no increase in the mobility of those who work in the higher-ranked institutions, where both management and employees seem to prefer the traditional life-time employment system. The definition of a change of employment in Japan was in terms of 'soiling one's *curriculum vitae*', and no doubt this native moral orientation was closely related to the fact that the individual's group identification is formed during the fairly early stages of his career, and that the individual's loyalty towards a group (always one particular group to which an individual gives his primary concern) also develops early.

There is an excellent recent example of this sociological orientation. Two leading companies, A and B, both partly engaged in the same sector of industry, established a new company by merging an equal part of the parent company, contributing an identical sum of capital, the same number of executive staff and workers, and so on. The internal system of the new company was arranged with the utmost care so that those joining from each parent company might enjoy an equal share and identical rights in its operation; thus a man from A was put at the head of X division, and a man from B came in as his deputy, while the head of Y division was a man from B and his deputy a man from A, and so on. However, the functional power of the new company was extremely low, for it was torn by each man's loyalty to his original company. In spite of the bright prospects for the efforts of the top organizers from both companies, there seemed little hope that a new, combined spirit would emerge. Rather, men's minds went back to the original company from which they came, and their efforts were always meant for their original company, in the hope that, one day, they might be allowed to return to the original company in return for their contributions to it during their stay in the new company. The top managers of both companies had been fully agreed on the mutual economic advantages to be gained from the establishment of the new company; but they had not been aware of, or had failed to take account of, the deep sociological and psychological orientation of their employees. For them, this had been a transfer to a less advantageous post, since in their reckoning the new company was so much lower in prestige than the original. In addition, they found it hard work alongside men who had breathed a different air for so long and, in place of a spirit of co-operation, there developed one of mutual hostility. Now it is envisaged that the new company cannot be made to work ideally until about twenty years hence – after the retirement of those who joined from the original companies and when the majority of the labour force is composed of those who have entered the new company from the start.

The firm attachment to a group by which he was employed in his early career contributes a great deal to a man's social recognition. This entails loyalty towards the group and hostility to other groups. If the other group is smaller and ranked lower one tends to look down on its members. This is well exemplified in the case of a merger between companies. A fairly recent case is the merger of Nissan (a leading automobile group) and Prince (a smaller company). It has been openly recognized by those concerned that the men of Prince are looked down on by the men of Nissan in the new merged company, and that the very good engineers and executives of the old Prince Company have suffered intolerable humiliation. Given such a social tendency, it becomes important for a man to enter a better group or institution in the earlier stages of his career. It is no exaggeration to say that the status of the company by which a man is employed governs the scope of his potential. Access to such employment depends largely on effort and good fortune in his youth rather than on his family background or wealth.

Throughout Japanese social history, chance meetings and the establishment of strong personal links at an early stage have often had great significance for a man's success. One born in a lower stratum who had the luck to become acquainted with a promising man has often attained success, while a man born in a high family often ends up unsuccessful. In other words, a man's attachment and hopes are often directed to his *kobun* rather than to his own sons or kinsmen. In fact, position or status are not monopolized by a particular family or status group, for the individual position or status in the vertical line is based on direct personal relations with others, and a man's position is rarely handed on to anyone not directly linked with him in his work. There have been many cases of a father in a distinguished position nominating one of his direct subordinates as his successor over his own son's head; the son, thus passed over may find his career outside his father's establishment or may receive a kind of pension from his father's business, or he may remain as a subordinate of the man who has succeeded his father. Indeed, many businesses are run by a man who is known by the traditional title *bantō* (which means, literally, a caretaker: in the modern system a *bantō* holds a top post such as the president or director of a company): he is usually the most senior subordinate of the deceased man, and often succeeds to the business over the heads of the sons and nephews of the deceased man.

This pattern of succession was to be found in many traditional business enterprises; it is not merely a feature of the contemporary industrial world. There have been many instances of a successor marrying his master's daughter, and becoming the legally entitled 'son-in-law' (see pp. 5–6). Of course the top post is often transmitted from a father to his own son, who has been trained and has worked with the father – not solely in virtue of the relationship. But in such cases the son is likely to face uneasy personal relations with men who are senior to him and had attached themselves directly to his father, whose loyalty towards his father cannot easily be shifted to the son. The son must have his own *kobun*, even when he succeeds to his father's business, and this results in changes in the power structure at the top of the group, thus leaving the way open for a new man to acquire power.

Even in the system of the Tokugawa Shogunate, which appears to be stable and rigid, there was much mobility among leading *samurai* families as a result of this mechanism. The son of a powerful Minister often failed to succeed to his father's status or office; but the son of a man of minor status might achieve great success and rise to a high post in the Shogunate. This kind of mobility, rather than being the result of intrigues among powerful families, was in part the outcome of a man's own achievement through personality and capability, and in part also could have been the effect of some chance, such as selection to be one of the child-companions to the successor of the Shōgun. It was the usual procedure for the young Shōgun, succeeding to his father's office, to appoint his own personal companions to important posts in the Shogunate, while old men who had held power through his father's favours gradually disappeared from the scene.

An identical pattern of inter-generational mobility is to be seen among modern Japanese political élites. To a large degree this is the basic pattern applying in various modern professional fields, though the modes and institutions of recruitment are, of course, different and more impersonal. This notable mobility often corroborates the standard Japanese social image of the rich man's son who is foolish, incapable and ready to dissipate the wealth which his father accumulated; and the poor man's son who is diligent and successful. There is a saying that the first generation acquires wealth, the second generation enjoys the father's status and exhausts his wealth, and the third generation reverts to poverty. Achievement of great social and economic success by a man born into a very poor family stands very high among the Japanese virtues.

Japan's modern educational system contributes a great deal towards this kind of mobility. The parent's prayer, 'Because I could not go to college or university and I ended up at the bottom of the barrel, I wish to have my children succeed', is probably stronger in Japan than in any other society. Going to a university, and specifically to a good university, is accepted as the prime prerequisite for upward mobility. The crucial importance of Japan's educational system derives from its weighty social implications.

In the traditional employment system in Japan, which reflects the general Japanese attitude to educational qualifications, the ability of an individual has been translated directly and simply in terms of his educational qualifications. Both length and quality of education are relevant criteria. By such standards, a man with only qualifications up to high-school level, whatever his ability and experience, cannot compete with a university graduate in obtaining employment or in climbing the promotion ladder. Three or four years in earlier life make a significant difference in Japan. Indeed, society in general regards educational background as one of the most important yardsticks of ability and social significance, and there is little regard for what a man has done outside school education. This kind of attitude is the product of the same soil that developed the seniority system, as has been discussed in detail above. Educational qualifications are obvious and perceivable, and can be used as a clear measurement and open indication, while it is difficult for everyone to agree on generally accepted and acknowledged standards to judge individual experience and achievements outside school. (This point was emphasized in the course of interviews with managers facing difficulties in shifting from the seniority system to a merit system.) As has been indicated already, Japanese methods of measurement are directed towards neat institutionalization; clearly perceptible criteria are given more weight than individual merit. It is within this frame that educational institutions play an exceedingly important rôle, in that they offer the individual social values and define his future potentiality in society.

Such considerations lead not only to a clear distinction between university graduates and high-school leavers but also to the development of a ranking order among the same categories of schools, the mechanism of which has already been discussed. The crystallization of the ranking order is at its clearest at university level, in that here is formed a direct link to the acquisition of a job.

The way in which a university plays an important rôle in determining the place of an individual in Japanese society is well illustrated by the normal undergraduate procedure and progress. The university entrance examination is an open and free competition, and universities, particularly those of the highest rank, resist any form of bribery or special favour. The wealth, status and so on of parents are completely disregarded (though this is not always so in the case of second-rate universities). Admission to a university by success in its entrance examination places an individual firmly within a somewhat caste-like system. Among the students of the University of Tokyo, for example, there are probably sons of farmers, workers, wealthy businessmen and professors, but they stand on a completely equal footing simply *because* they gained entry into the University of Tokyo; and ever after they belong to a kind of social clique as 'graduates of the University of Tokyo'. The existence of university cliques in Japan is so well developed that they may indeed sometimes have a function comparable to that of a caste group in India, in terms of a monopoly of certain privileges through mobilizing, in a helpful fashion, friendships and relationships that are able to cut across departmental and institutional divisions. They do not form any overtly distinctive group; clique consciousness is felt more by those outside the group than those inside it. But that some covert advantages accrue to clique members becomes evident in their relatively easy access to employment after graduation.

The rank of the university from which he has graduated more or less determines the range of an individual's activities, the accessibility of certain levels of status and the degree of success he may expect for the rest of his life. There is a tendency, becoming increasingly obvious in recent years, for the highest-ranking industrial plant or business firm to recruit its graduate intake from the highest-ranked university. Today this tendency is becoming so strong that, as has been mentioned already, top-ranking companies limit applications strictly to the new graduates of top-ranking universities.

Once employed, a man tends to remain in the same institution until his retirement. Few graduates leave the institution in which they took their first job; they simply step up the ladder to a higher position within the system. In comparison with inter-generational mobility, horizontal mobility (movement from one institution to another) is exceedingly limited. In other words, opportunities for upward manoeuvre are confined to the period of entering a university. Thus entry to the highest-rated universities opens direct access to the royal road; this is even more true today than in the time of our fathers and grandfathers, since, with the rise of economic standards, there is an increase in the number of those able to go to university, which produces more intense competition between and a more strictly defined hierarchical order among universities. This helps to explain the severity of competition for entrance to the top universities. The chances of entry into a top-ranking university are enhanced if one applies from a high school of repute – and so on down to the primary school.

Thus, schooling in Japan involves more intense competition than in most other societies. This may help to explain the annual repetition of the tragic news story of the suicides of one or two young students after failure in the entrance examination of the University of Tokyo. Though it may be that such students are not normal, the event is still interpreted as a symbol of the very heavy social pressures upon young boys. It is also not difficult to understand why Japanese who graduate (or even receive a PhD) from universities abroad rather than from universities in Japan fail to secure appointment to good posts in leading Japanese institutions. Such foreign products are somewhat alien and are pushed aside, in that they do not fit the hierarchy of the Japanese social system. The acquisition of additional training or experience in higher institutions abroad certainly offers advantage and prestige, but it is more important that one must be well set on the royal road of the Japanese system.

In various fields in Japan, particularly in the business sector, international dealings are increasing rapidly and creating the need for personnel trained and experienced in such dealings. Every institution tackles this problem in the same way – by sending promising young employees, who have been through Japanese education to university level, for additional training to educational institutions in the west; this is in preference to employing those who have already, by their own initiative, had previous training or experience abroad. Managers say that their chosen method produces personnel of a much higher quality. It is interesting to note that this has been the traditional method of foreign study since the beginning of Japan's modernization. An examination of the list of Japanese studying abroad over the last hundred years shows that those who took the major rôles in the development of modern Japan after returning from a period of study abroad are on the whole those who were sent abroad deliberately at government expense or under the auspices of business institutions.

Here is further evidence that the basic social and political system of modern Japan was already firmly established at the start of the process of modernization. It can be argued that the basic system of modern Japan was inherited from the previous Tokugawa regime and that the modern changes of the Meiji period, which appear so drastic, occurred without any structural change in terms of the basic state configuration. This is why, in part, Japan was able to attain such a pitch of industrialization so swiftly; if there had been the need to change the structural configuration the disorder caused by the restructuring of the fundamental system would have lowered the speed of the process and would have brought far greater suffering. In other words, the wheels of the vehicle had been made long before modernization, and it required only changes in the type of passenger carried and the direction taken. It has been fashionable for the Japanese to look at modernization from the start as a process that has been (or should be) based on and effected by a combination of the Japanese spirit and western knowledge (*wakno-yōsai*). Instead of such an idealistic view, modernization should be seen in terms of the structure of the political and social configuration: modernization has been carried out not by changing the traditional structure but by utilizing it. In concrete form, the structure consists of the highly centralized administrative system, vertical organization of groups and so on.

Education plays an important rôle in contributing to the very high systemization of various institutions in modern Japan. Employment with a foreign firm in Japan is regarded somehow as out of the system. In spite of the very high salary, very few well-qualified men are ready to take a job in these firms. This reluctance comes first from the feeling of insecurity about the future. Secondly, foreign firms are somehow beyond the pale of Japanese social recognition, so that their employees are likely to be regarded as not part of the Japanese community; this is something not to be readily tolerated by a Japanese. Since

Japanese society is so well structured, the individual man locates himself in the system; the feeling involved is perhaps comparable to that of citizenship in western societies. The system bifurcates in complex and delicate ways, but the major pattern is unmistakably perceived by each individual, and the particular part around and involving him is at least very clear to him. This sociological systematization has become more and more obvious as Japan's industrialization proceeds and as the number of what the Japanese call *sarariman* (salaried men or in Whyte's term, 'organization men') has increased to occupy the major and dominant positions in society. Given such a sociological setting, these modern Japanese organization men hardly conceive of themselves as the same new race or class as do their American counterparts. Sociologists toss around terms such as 'white-collar' or 'middle class', and the Japanese organization men call themselves *sarariman*, yet they are reluctant or not yet ready to be looked on as a group or stratum. They are concerned, rather, with the company for which they work and, according to their own concepts, they are aligned in various cliques arranged hierarchically.

The group, with a high degree of isolation from the outside, and a rigid hierarchical structure internally, offers its members security for life, but tends to ignore the dynamics which will accommodate differences of individual quality. This system is, therefore, best suited to the group in which members are of roughly the same standard and where the nature of the work required does not call for any high degree of individual specialist merit. The Japanese civil service, in fact, fulfils these various qualifications. Civil servants are screened by a national examination and have the reputation of being the group at the top, at least as far as Japanese education can train a man; the majority of them are found in the graduates of the Faculty of Law in the University of Tokyo, which is recognized informally as the highest-ranking faculty in Japan's most prestigious university. The promotion system is of the escalator type, and there are sufficient posts available for frequent and equal opportunities of promotion.

Within this system, Japanese civil servants manifest the characteristics of Japanese group consciousness. They do not, as in the case of members of the Indian Administrative Service, form a caste-like group which is open to and ranges through their whole membership; rather, they develop very strong in-group feelings dividing ministry from ministry and even departments within a ministry. In fact, relationships between ministries and even between departments of the same ministry are often extremely poor. There is a highly sensitive consciousness of seniority, determined by the year in which the national examination was taken. There is also a well-recognized and universally acknowledged ranking order of the various ministries. So there is considerable concern for individual, departmental or ministry seniority which blunts sensitivity to the privilege common to the service as a whole. This is a collection of able men, confident and sure of success, the self-confidence being the more sure in the higher ranked ministries.

This is the most comfortable career of all for the Japanese. A man reaches the highest available post open to him and, soon afterwards, retires. As they approach the highest post, such as a vice-minister, the number of posts becomes extremely limited. It is the custom that all members of the year group (formed by the year when they passed the national examination) in the same ministry will resign when one of them is appointed vice-minister. They are only just past the age of fifty and, like beautiful girls of marriageable age, are open to many attractive offers. These are mainly from firms with which they have dealt during their official service, for it pays a private firm in Japan to have its close links with government; a newly retired civil servant, who has just occupied high office, is therefore an attractive proposition.

The career of the professional is, by contrast, far from an easy one. There are wide differences in individual merit, and the number of high posts with reputable status is limited. To succeed as a scholar, for example, one must get a university post, in a high-ranking university. The number of such posts is limited, particularly as once a man is appointed (in his twenties, usually) he will stay a member of his department until his retirement, regardless of the calibre or quantity of his research. Applications for vacancies caused by retirement are normally only considered from graduates of the university in question and, as the selection of candidates is at departmental level, the voices of a narrow group at the top become very influential. Unless a professor or head of department is distinguished and broad-minded, he is most unlikely to select someone stronger (academically as well as in personality) than himself.

So departments or institutes within the top-ranking universities do not necessarily possess the best available scholars; in fact, the competent scholars often fail to reach the best posts. This phenomenon is not confined to the universities; it is to be found in almost all the professions in Japan. There are informal hierarchical groups which militate against opportunities for free competition on the basis of individual merit.

Probably the worst situation is to be found in the fields of modern fine art and music, where, ideally, the nature of the work demands free competition. The difficulties arise from the survival of the *iemoto* system (see pp. 60–61), for artists today are recruited into the system which functions latently in modern school organization. Social recognition of a man's proficiency derives from the link with his teacher, rather than from free competition based on talent. This system tends to blur differences in individual merit, since, once a personal relation is established between a teacher and a student, the teacher seldom dismisses his student, in that the teacher's prestige (and his income also) rises in proportion to the number of students under him. Students attached to a teacher compete with each other for their teacher's favour – which is the only way for them to acquire fame – and in such competition they often employ means other than proficiency in their art. Therefore a man who is really talented may fail in his career because of poor relations with his teacher and colleagues, or because of the relative weakness of the group to which his teacher belongs, in comparison with other competing groups. Moreover, the *iemoto* system may offer great handicaps to proper training, in that a pupil may not approach teachers in other areas or groups. Although such an approach is theoretically possible, it may well entail loss of his teacher's favour, on the grounds that his loyalty to the latter is made suspect.

A group often disregards its best or most promising member; inter-group relations and communications are so poor that the best members of a profession may well be isolated from each other and general standards dragged down. These factors have lowered the standards of professional activity in Japan, for the concern given to institutional framework detracts from the attention that should be paid to the recognition of professional merit. The professional man in Japan ranks lower than in the western social scale and, in fact, even the concept of 'the professions' is far from distinct. Instead, the professional man is regarded as a member of a certain institution and is disregarded unless his institution is well known and of high status. If an academic, for example, is respectable and of repute it is rather because his chair is at a university of repute than because of the distinction of his research.

The effect of these factors is often considerable. In journalism, for example, there are virtually no 'free-lances'; a journalist is known as a member of A Paper or Z Press, which he joined after leaving university and with which he stays until retirement. Entrants work as reporters for the first ten years or so and then begin the climb to supervising positions, becoming established personnel in their organization. But the writing of first-hand reports is not regarded in Japan as a fitting occupation for an established man, so such work is either farmed out to cub reporters or is given over to well-known academics, professional writers and social critics. Senior and competent journalists rarely sign or contribute articles, for the higher status or popularity of the academic or the critic brings greater competitive power to the newspaper which signs them up. The journalist in Japan does not have the status of his counterpart in the West: he is a caretaker of others' writings rather than a writer himself, and, as such, a member of a profession.

A white-collar career in industry and business – the road to the executive's office – comes mid-way between the civil service and the professions. The advantages of the civil servant are lacking, in that there is not a consistent standard of behaviour or hierarchy to be followed; on the other hand, there is not the degree of disorder that is found in the world of the professions. Again, in that the aim is profit-making, management is more efficient than in the government sector, and greater regard is given to individual merit. Even so, as has been indicated before, there are major difficulties in the way of the application of a merit system; recruitment is open usually only to those who are finishing their education and there is a reluctance to employ those who have already worked elsewhere, except in the case of a new and rapidly expanding organization. Because 'white-collar' executive jobs are highly valued, Japanese organizations suffer from a surplus of staff in administrative posts and indeed, one of the major concerns of forward-looking managers is the problem of the reduction of administrative personnel.

This society gives precedence to the institutional system over individual quality. The workings of this system produce evenness of quality and may help to raise the standards of those who would be passed over in another system. But the system fails to cope satisfactorily with those whose ability is the greatest. This failure accords with the readiness of the Japanese to think of himself in terms of his group and to forget the matter of individual autonomy. Critics have pointed out, since the early days of Japan's modernization, that Japan cannot press her claims to have modernized until individual autonomy is given greater recognition. But it is interesting to observe that the traditional system, manifested in group organization, has generated both the major driving force towards a high degree of industrialization and the negative brake which hinders the development of individual autonomy.

2. The web of comradeship

Since the Japanese man, after the end of his education, spends his life within the same group or institution, his comrades are naturally to be found within or around his place of work. With rare exceptions, the Japanese man has a close set of individuals whom he may call 'my group' or 'my friends', distinct from the immediate family with whom he shares his daily living. As was outlined in Chapter One, the institution or association to which he belongs is perceived as the group to which the conceptual extension of his household is applied, and he normally has a single loyalty towards this group. His conception of his 'own' group is sharpened when he meets other people. As an appropriate example, if one listens to a conversation between Japanese one does not have to wait long to hear the words *uchi-no* or *uchi-dewa*, referring to one's own people and work place. *Uchi* may mean an institution as a whole, or it may mean the department or section to which the speaker belongs. It is common for an individual to belong to a certain informal group (which is often a faction within a larger group), and this is the group of primary and most intimate concern in his social life. The bases for the formation of such a group may be found in congenial friendship, long and stable association through work; common backgrounds, such as being graduates of the same high school or college, can also be an important factor in conjunction with friendship.

An individual's social contacts are usually confined to the limits of the circle or place of work where he has daily contacts. Thus the setting of the institution has importance as the base which defines the individual's social world. With his social environment so limited, the scope of an individual's relations within his own group becomes proportionately more intensified. Obligations and expectations among the members of the group are exacting; members of a group know each other exceedingly well – one's family life, love affairs, even the limits of one's capacity for cocktails are intimately known to the others.

125

Among fellow-members a single word would suffice for the whole sentence. The mutually sensitive response goes so far that each easily recognizes the other's slightest change in behaviour and mood and is ready to react accordingly.

Just how much a Japanese depends on, and expects from, his friends may be incomprehensible to the outsider. There are no clear lines which divide one's own from another's responsibility, and the sentiments embodied in the English expression, 'That is (not) your (my) business', strike a Japanese as cold indeed. In contrast, 'I understand how you are placed', or, 'Leave it to me: I will do it as best I can for you', and so on, are familiar and welcome to the Japanese.

The deep involvement in personal relations within one's work group may have the advantage of giving social and psychological security to those who have moved from a traditional community to become urban residents. The majority do not usually belong to any intimate social group outside the place of work, but they feel neither so lonely nor so estranged as workers in the West might feel in similar conditions, for in Japan workplace friendships usually extend to private life.

A group such as this, based on the workplace, has indeed a very similar function and rôle to that of a *mura*, a traditional rural village community. A man becomes secure through tightly knit communal activities. In return, he must always adjust himself to group demands and accept the group consensus, even though it might seem unreasonable both in content and method of presentation. If he insists on opposing it, even if his opinion is reasonable and correct, he would risk being cast out from the group. Within his group he is secure, but his security is maintained at the expense of his individual autonomy.

The Japanese man thus develops friendships primarily with his fellow workers in the same section or department of an institution. Coupled with or cutting across such an institutional group, a man has a set of specially close friends, who may be his *sempai*, *kōhai* or *dōryō* in his present or a previous place of work. The network of friendships so formed often cuts across the formal sectional organization of an institution, since an individual can be transferred from one section to another, though, on the whole, a group of this kind tends to be formed among the *uchi-no* people within one institution. If members of the group do not belong to the same place of work they at least know about each other's work and activities, so that they can be of ready assistance to each other. In his place of work a man may have to deal with *sempai, kōhai* and *dōryō* whom he does not like and with whom he may have trouble. Against these, his group of close friends stands as an ally and protection. Not only in crisis but also at lonely or unhappy points in daily life a man goes first to his fellows for consolation. Thus, as long as a man has such fellows, he is socially and emotionally secure.

If a man happened to make a mistake in his work his friends in the group would protect him. Even in a very serious case, where no reasonable excuse would justify his actions, they would protect him with the group power and fabricate some irrational and emotional justification. They are at all times firmly on his side, not necessarily because he is right but because he is one of them. His fellows know well enough that he has committed a fault and is in the wrong, but even so, they retain to a striking degree their tolerance and sympathy for him. An accusation serious enough to lead to loss of career may well arise out of a man's unhappy personal relations with his fellows rather than from the actual weight of his misdemeanour. One could point to many cases in which a man had committed a serious error and had even broken the law (and would have lost his position in another society), but remained comfortably in his post in spite of social accusations on the part of the general public. At worst, he might be transferred to a different post until the temperature of public opinion might cool. Rational judgement and universal rules defer to personal relationships. Even modern law and healthy public opinion have to compromise with such strong group manipulation. Hence the origin of incomprehensible and destructive intrigues and factional rivalries.

The existence of such a strong in-group feeling with a high emotional content which disregards objective intellectual observation and analysis of individual qualities seems to be related to the difficulty facing the establishment of a merit system in Japan. As has been said, the application of a merit system in place of one based on seniority is no easy measure; recent attempts, particularly in industrial enterprises, have had results that are generally quite disappointing. One of the problems seems to lie in the difficulty in operating a fair and objective judgement of individual quality, for the readiness to evaluate an individual on the basis of subjective impressions means that, as a general rule, a Japanese will pay more attention to and find greater interest in personality than capability. Personal impressions often condition judgements of merit, so that a merit system may be open to opportunities for favouritism and discrimination on the part of the senior man towards his subordinates. It may be partly because of this that the seniority system, along with the classification of school careers and so on, has gained such a firm foothold in the Japanese employment system.

The high degree of involvement in inter-personal relationships of both positive (allies) and negative (enemies) kinds within such small groups must surely be allied to, though perhaps not the cause of, the development of the extremely sensitive manners, phraseology (virtually incapable of translation), facial expressions and postures of the Japanese. The delicacy tends to be couched in ambiguity of expression, which is used to avoid confrontation, for self-defence and to conceal hostility. The flattery, the insinuation and the smile are used to gain advantages, while at the same time they conceal the precise nature of desire or feeling. On the other hand, irrational or mischievous conduct is used to spite others. (The highly developed standards in the practices of delicacy may be compared with the Italian art of flattery and the techniques of English cunning.)

The acquisition of these extremely delicate ways of conducting personal relations requires considerable social training, though most Japanese achieve them through their social life from childhood onwards. Not only foreigners but also even those Japanese who spend their teens or twenties abroad face considerable difficulty in meeting all the complicated techniques of personal relations, which do not require much intellectual manoeuvre but demand highly sensitive and nervous procedures. Indeed, these procedures involve a degree of nervous fatigue and expenditure of emotion not normally found in such measure in other societies.

This may give some understanding of the reason why the Japanese salaried man has such a great need for taverns and bars. The concentration of bars on back streets in the shopping centres of cities is extremely high in comparison with the cities of any other country. Each evening in Tokyo after the offices close many office workers stop at bars on their way home, and some of them remain drinking there until well after the last train. It is not the drink itself that attracts them so much as the chance of relaxation after the tension and competition in the office; bars are thought to be soothing to the nerves. The layout and atmosphere of these bars are quite different from the London pub, which from a Japanese point of view is big and impersonal, open and bustling. Japan's bars are mostly small, dimly lighted (but not so gloomy as in America), with a background of quiet mood music, and smart hostesses to serve clients' drinks and to listen with constant appreciation and ready sympathy to whatever he says. It is a very personal atmosphere: no matter how stupid a man is, he is accepted. To soothe his tired nerves, a man begins to crave bar madames (who satisfy, in a way, the mother complex of Japanese men) and bar girls (with a touch of temporary sweethearts), and drinking companions who can empathize with what he says and with his intense desires. The majority of bar conversations are about, and mostly against, the people in the same place of work; strategy and intrigues are often an important topic; love affairs, troubles in the family, personal experiences retailed boastfully – much of the talk is so stupid as to make one wonder that it can come from the lips of adult men. Surprisingly enough, many of them are intellectuals; a man's education or upbringing seems to have no bearing in this context.

It is Japanese tradition that whatever is said in drink is excused and should be forgotten. The bar is therefore important as a place to pour out all frustrations. Many Japanese will say without scruple, 'I can't live without a bar.' Such bars, along with madame and her girls, appear very frequently in hundreds of popular novels and cheap stories in Japan. Some western journalist, having noticed this phenomenon of 'bar culture', wrote a piece suggesting that because Japanese houses are small, men spend more time in bars. This is very far from the truth, for it has nothing to do with the size of the home. A bar has a function of its own, which cannot be replaced by home or mistress.

Indeed, conversation over drinks has a significant function for Japanese men, who are rather slow to speak out on formal occasions and feel considerable pressure from the rigid vertical system. When a formal meeting faces deadlock or when difficulties arise in personal relations a chat over drinks often proves effective. A gathering of intimate and life-long friends to drink together is one of the most enjoyable occasions for Japanese men; here they can find complete relaxation and can talk and laugh from the heart. At such gatherings, where the atmosphere is assisted by drinks, a sentence is never completed; the conversation may jump from one topic to another with no apparent linking theme; topics will be taken up at the whim of each speaker and in such rapid succession that an outsider may well be unable to catch even the general drift. The game is played in a succession of quick and timely reactions, interspersed with jokes which prompt immediate, boisterous laughter. Thus, the essence of pleasure in conversation for the Japanese is not in discussion (a logical game) but in emotional exchange; it is not easy for those who have different ideas and backgrounds to join profitably or successfully in such an exercise.

Japanese men enjoy such informal talks with friends in bars or restaurants rather than at home. The rhythm of their life is quite different from that of, for example, 'organization man' in America, who often holds parties at home, inviting his friends and their wives. Japanese 'organization man' finds it burdensome to arrange the date for such an invitation well beforehand; he prefers to spend an informal evening with his friends on impulse when the day's work is over. There is also, of course, a kind of uneasiness in talking with friends in the presence of the respective wives.

A man tends always to drink with the same group, gathered from *sempai* and *kōhai* who are similar in age and rank; close *dōryō*, who stand in a relationship of rivalry, tend to be excluded. The relationship between man and bar, also, tends to remain fairly constant; a man will be a regular visitor to the same bar where he can drink without cash payment. Thus a man spends not only the working hours but many evenings of relaxation in company with his colleagues; such close intimacy between working colleagues leads to the development of cliques and complicates the processes of decision-making. If ever a Japanese invites others to his home it is these working colleagues; in much the same way a Japanese peasant would never broaden his circle of friendships beyond the village community. Neighbours rarely become friends unless the local community is long established and childhood and former school friends remain in the immediate area. Mere neighbourliness or the similarity of living patterns as organization men would not be a sufficient basis for friendship. New suburban communities do not provide the essentials for friendship (see pp. 63–4); a man is too deeply involved in the affairs of his place of work to have time or inclination to make friends in his neighbourhood, and home for him is the place of rest, not the centre of social activities. Wives may make friends with neighbours, but because husbands are reluctant to join in these associations, they remain partial and shallow. Standards of living and income levels may be similar, but the differences in the husbands' places of work hinders the progress of such wives' associations.

In such a society the wife tends to be shut out from any social activities and her attention is directed to her own children. The mother's excessive care for her children is often found fault with by social critics; but this phenomenon is closely linked with the situation facing women in the newly established or developing communities where most organization men make their home. These wives and mothers lack access to any means of extending their social activities; they live far away from parents, brothers and sisters and schoolfriends. For them, the ideal husband should return home as soon as his work is over, and should take his wife and children for an outing on Sunday. The new family ideology has been called *my-home-ism*; it implies that the husband should regard his family as of supreme importance and spend as much time with them as possible. Even so, this new trend has not produced a new family pattern centred on the relationship between husband and wife. Rather, the structure of the family is based on a central core, mother and children, to which husband (father) attaches. For the husband, the object of concern is the home as a whole, rather than his wife and his children as individuals. This is indeed the traditional concept of *'ie'* or *'uchi'*, with the 'household' usually now restricted in scope to include only his wife and his children.

My-home-ism keeps husband, wife and children together, but relationships between families are very weak: hence, the husband has very few social obligations as the household head, and finds it all the easier to concentrate his attention on the affairs of his place of work. A man's attention to his wife and children decreases as he climbs the promotion ladder and becomes more involved in the affairs of his place of work – and the after-hours visits to bars and restaurants. The Japanese husband appears far more free than his western counterpart and, on this account, Japanese wives come in for their fair share of sympathy. But the average middle-aged Japanese wife does not appear to need such sympathy; she will often say something such as, 'How fortunate it is to have a husband who is healthy and at work' (in other words, absent from the home). In fact, most Japanese wives adopt the rôle of mother rather than wife to their husbands; this is the traditional pattern, little affected by post-war change. The core of the Japanese family, ancient and modern, is the parent–child relationship, not that between husband and wife. So the family today also reflects the predominance of vertical relationships.

The Japanese man makes only occasional contacts with his relatives, and these usually because of his wife's demands. He will visit his wife's parents and siblings more regularly than his own, and, in cases of difficulty (shortage of money, unemployment, etc.), the traditional practice is to go to his wife's parents (or send her to them) rather than his own parents or brothers. Actual relationships with relatives tend to be closer on the wife's side, although the husband's relatives are accorded precedence on formal occasions.

Apart from relationships deriving from the place of work, education creates more effective relationships than kinship. The 'school clique' (*gakubatsu* – a commonly used term) denotes the group consciousness deriving mainly from a common university or college background. Graduates of the same university or college share an in-group feeling, a ready familiarity in face of others. A common educational background comes next to institution or place of work in degree of function and is more effective than either family or local background. The 'school clique' would come into function in the case of an interview, for example, where, other counts being equal, it proved difficult to choose between candidates. In the early years of Japan's modernization, in the late nineteenth century, the locality, in terms of the territory of a former feudal lord, for example, played an important part in the development of cliques and the advantages they brought; today, although local background is still effective, it is by no means as vital as the 'school clique', particularly at the level of the organization man.

The network of the 'school clique' offers advantages inside and outside the place of work. When the institution is large and includes a number of university graduates 'school cliques' may be formed latently within it. Further, within each clique there is the recognized order of *sempai-kōhai* and class-mates, which again contributes a kind of group feeling to tie these members to each other, so that they do feel a kind of mutual familiarity denied to others. If his school is among the higher ranked, a man's school contemporaries are also likely to be climbing successfully the ladders of other institutions, so that they are able to render mutual services when needed. However, the function of the 'school clique' network is conditioned by differences in occupation and the difference in status of the institutions in which members are employed. Even between class-mates, one who works in a minor company will develop a kind of inferiority complex towards a friend in a well-known large company, so that the relationship will become much weaker than that between class-mates who are equally successful in comparable fields. Hence, a 'school clique' is not a distinguishable functional group, all members of which enjoy similar and regular rights; rather, it offers advantages in utilizing relationships when the need arises. The relationship often works very effectively in a manner comparable to that of Hindu caste fellowmen, or Chinese lineage members. The effectiveness of the relationship is particularly pronounced among graduates of the same department, since they can easily trace vertical links and so recognize clearly the relative status of *sempai* and *kōhai*. If we equate university department with lineage group the university as a whole is comparable with the clan (in its structural sense rather than at organizational level).

If a man has a network of friendships outside his immediate place of work it is usually that of his 'school clique'. In scope, in density of personal relationship and in availability, 'school clique' relationships function more effectively than kinship. This is another reason why those educated outside Japan are handicapped in their careers: on the other hand, a foreigner who has been educated in Japan is accepted as a member of the group and can enjoy and make use of in-group feelings. Birth and colour do not evoke as much prejudice as school or institution in Japan; the sharing of experience during the critical period of the teens and twenties has life-long effects.

There is here a close link with the concept of the 'household' (*ie*). *De jure* membership of a traditional rural community is acquired primarily through the 'household', and the individual is classified as the son of X household, rather than as the son of X parents. Again, it was normal practice for a household without a son to adopt; once adopted, whether he had a kinship relation with the household head or not, he could enjoy the full rights of membership of the household, just as if he were the true son of the household head. The 'school clique' is based on the same conceptual root as the traditional *ie*; there is a close link, also, with the principles on which members of the same place of work or institution form their groups. To acquire membership, one should have shared activities in the same institution over a certain period. Here, it becomes obvious why the place of work is important in the formation of comradeship, for, under the Japanese employment system, it is this institution to which a man commits himself deeply, and almost irrevocably, from his early twenties.

3. Localism and tangibility

The social organization which causes an individual to be engrossed so deeply in personal relations at the same time limits the scope of his personal relations. He is well informed about his own group and institution, and to a somewhat lesser extent about those in competition. But his activities and concerns rarely extend beyond this world.

The extreme delicacy of demeanour mentioned earlier is chiefly applied to, and functions among, the 'own' group. The Japanese have failed to develop any social manner properly applicable to strangers, to people from 'outside'. In the store of Japanese etiquette there are only two basic patterns available: one which applies to a 'superior' and another which applies to an 'inferior'; or, to put it another way, there are expressions of familiarity and expressions of hostility, but none which apply on the peer level or which indicate indifference. This produces discomfort during contact with a stranger, whether he be foreigner or Japanese.

The Japanese are often thought by foreigners to be very reserved. A more accurate description would be that Japanese on the whole are *not sociable*. This is partly because, once outside their immediate orbit, they are at a loss for appropriate forms of expression. They have not developed techniques for dealing with persons 'outside', because their lives are so tightly concentrated into their 'own' groups. Within these groups, the Japanese could not be described as reserved. In virtue of the sense of unity fostered by the activities and emotions of the group, each member is shaped to more or less the same mould, and forced to undergo the kneading effects of group interaction whether he likes it or not. The individual Japanese has little opportunity to learn sociability. Whatever security he feels is derived from aligning and matching himself with group purpose and plan; his circle is all he knows, and there is little real functional value in mere socializing. He may thus go through life without experiencing the pleasures and strains of 'extra-mural contests'. Even if individuality is not entirely submerged, at the very least the chances of cultivating it are very strictly limited.

Such circumstances affect the character of interpersonal relationships; they are 'tangible' and strongly 'local'. Localism characterizes all fields of activity. A politician, for example, will join a particular faction and will remain there for life; once he has committed himself, his personal success or failure thereafter are bound up with the success or failure of his faction. There is no avenue for transfer to another faction. Even channels of communication between factions are very poor, so much so that it is said that the only medium for the exchange of information is the well-trained political news correspondent, who thus occupies an important linking position. The political group has developed its own peculiar world, into which hardly anyone could be, or would care to be, admitted (unless he is prepared to be accepted at the bottom of the hierarchy) and politicians are regarded as a breed somewhat apart.

In contemporary Japan it is very rare for a professor, for example, to become a government minister. Each institutional group is firmly fenced in, and no individual can pass freely over this fence. This tendency has grown more and more since the earlier stage of Japan's modernization. The institutionalization of modern Japanese society has been so thorough and pervasive that those from differing occupations feel uneasy even in conversation, since they are deeply concerned with their own group and are ignorant of any other. A conversation between a scholar and a diplomat, for example, would be found by both to be dull, unstimulating and superficial. The early specialization of the individual (as soon as he has finished school) and his isolation within his respective group – together with the life-employment system, which puts the individual into an airtight chamber and allows him no chance to breathe the outside air – these and similar factors eliminate or reduce the common ground which would be the basis of intellectual discussion in spite of the difference of occupational and institutional background.

There is little inter-communication between intellectuals in different occupations and institutions. There is not even a newspaper or magazine read by Japanese intellectuals as a whole, and although there have been several attempts to create a daily newspaper catering specifically for intellectuals, they have always ended in failure. There are several magazines directed at the intellectual, but none of these has succeeded, as their western counterpart has usually done, in reaching a broad spectrum of the intellectual sector of Japanese society. In fact, articles and discussions in such magazines are seldom taken up by intellectuals as topics of everyday or casual conversation, for such articles generally take the form of a straightforward statement, a kind of one-way communication, which is intended, consciously or unconsciously, to level up the general intellectual standard. Hence, such magazines do not offer an ideal venue for intellectual games which contributor and reader alike may enjoy on an equal footing. So such magazines serve an educational rôle; in that they fail to offer intellectual enjoyment, they fail to reach and satisfy a wide range of intellectuals.

In fact, it is difficult to draw a line between intellectuals and the general mass, for the intellectual stratum is not clearly differentiated. The absence of any common ground among Japanese intellectuals may also assist the workings of the mechanism by which intellectuals are scattered into numerous mutually exclusive and closed groups.

The formation of groups occurs not only at the occupational level but also at various minor levels; again, smaller groups may be formed within a minor group. Among scholars, specialists in a particular field may be formed into groups divided according to school loyalties; these may be segmented into smaller sub-groups which come together on the basis of more intimate relations. It is this smallest group that has the significant function; its core may consist of several scholars who share a common view and style of approach, derived from a single ruling theory. A group normally has its central figure to whom the other members attach, often emotionally, on the basis of former professor–student or classmate relationships. A grouping of this nature, as with politicians, serves as a protection of the weaker, who might be forgotten or unproductive if forced back solely on their own resources. But this group structure has drawbacks in the development of science, for instance; group members meet very frequently, but rarely do they discuss issues with persons outside their group. In the course of time each group devises and promulgates its own peculiar styles of expression and parochial terms, not understandable to the outsider even though he works in the same field of specialization. Such obstacles to productive discussion make it difficult for scholar-groups in Japan even to reach mutual understanding.

If, even among themselves, Japanese specialists have difficulties in communication, in the domain of international affairs they find their problems compounded. One of the best-known political scientists, who leads a large group of disciples, confessed recently on his return from Europe and America that foreigners' problems are so different from *ours* that he could not easily communicate with them. (It is my contention that he can speak only for himself and his group, not for Japanese specialists as a whole. However, this is indeed a difficulty for many Japanese scholars, and particularly for those who specialize in the social sciences.)

Curricula and standards of teaching in Japanese higher education are not very different from those of western countries. The difficulty facing scholars arises from the insularity which they themselves have occasioned, for Japan as a nation experiences this same localism because of the handicap of the lack of direct interchange with other intellectual peoples, and because of the curbs on exchange imposed by the Japanese language itself. These problems are also derived, oddly enough, from the high standard of education in Japan. If Japan were much more backward a considerable number of Japan's intellectuals would have sought training abroad, and could therefore help to overcome localism among other Japanese intellectuals. In fact, our predecessors of the Meiji period, who did study abroad, were much more international in spirit than the intellectuals of today. The localism which is in some degree inescapable by the Japanese has been accentuated and aggravated by the intellectuals themselves in virtue of the artificial insulation deriving from idiosyncratic group jargon.

Thus, the localism, which has its roots mainly in the social structure, meets the emotional needs of the individual who seeks security within the group, and compensates for his lack of individual autonomy. The general tendency of the majority of Japanese, as is so strongly evidenced by the modern intellectual, is to seek security rather than autonomy.

To cite one example, the holiday pleasure tours which have become highly fashionable among Japanese recently are invariably conducted in groups, composed of some thirty to fifty people, who belong to the same commercial association, company, village or the like. Smaller groups may be formed from among friends or members of a family. It is extremely rare for an individual to travel alone except in the case of business; a lone traveller may be considered rather unusual or odd.*

* Japanese inns are very reluctant to take in a traveller without companions. This reluctance comes partly from the standpoint of profit: in Japan an inn sets its charges at so much per person, rather than per room. A friend who loves travelling alone often complains that he has been refused accommodation in an inn when he arrived without a reservation, because he had no companions. It is even worse for a woman travelling alone; she would be thought brokenhearted, perhaps recently

Moreover, most Japanese dislike travelling alone because it induces a feeling of loneliness and psychological insecurity. This is not unrealistic, for a lone traveller in trouble could hardly expect help from 'outsiders' who did not know his face. Public mutual assistance, such as is to be found very readily in England, is only rarely evident in Japan. So, even on holiday trips, the Japanese surround themselves with friends or fellow workers, carrying with them their communal identity wherever they go. They rarely mix with the residents of the locality in which they travel, nor with others they encounter along the way.

These traits are also prevalent among Japanese abroad. Whether in the West or South-east Asia, the Japanese community tends to remain aloof from both the local people and other foreigners. Paradoxically, the rare Japanese who does develop a very close contact with local people will probably cut himself off from other Japanese in the community. In such action his localism has simply taken another direction, and this is surely to be expected, for it is wholly consistent with the one-way tendency in the Japanese character.

The *localism* which functions externally to preclude personal relationships with the 'outsider' produces internally distinct characteristics of the *tangibility* of personal relations. The structural requirement for overcoming the instability which stems from the varying natures of the group's constituents is, as has been said before, the promotion of group consciousness. Since this is usually kindled by an appeal to emotion, it necessitates tangible contact between people. Such contact must then be maintained by constant face-to-face activity so as to nurture the flame.

In Japanese society frequent meeting with friends and acquaintances is a general observed norm. The most common

divorced or at least someone not very sociable or happy. I myself do not have the courage to go to a Japanese inn without first making a reservation through some local person who can explain my status and my business to the proprietor; this makes a great difference in service and comfort. In contrast, I thoroughly enjoy a trip by myself in foreign countries.

phrase that is trundled out when Japanese acquaintances meet after some interval is, 'Excuse my not being able to have had the pleasure of meeting you earlier.' The frequency of meeting is regarded as a measure of the closeness and firmness of the relationship.

The relative strength of a bond between people tends to be proportional to the length and intensity of actual contact. The reason why a 'newcomer' to any Japanese group is placed at the very bottom of the hierarchy is that he has had the shortest period of contact. In this facet of group life is another breeding ground of the seniority system which dominates Japan more strikingly than nepotism in other societies. And when an individual's place in his group is governed solely by the length of his actual contact with the group, contact itself becomes the individual's private social capital. Because this capital is not transferable to any other group, the individual cannot shift from one group to another without undergoing very great social loss. Even if a man's company abandoned the seniority system and he could move to a new job at the same or a higher salary, so that a move entailed no actual economic loss, the social loss would remain (see pp. 109–10).

In conjunction with the factor of the absolute time span, an additional factor of temporary loss of tangibility may enter into the operation of the direct contact element. A group member who is absent temporarily may well lose ground within the group, for a period of separation often alienates existing contacts. When a man working in Tokyo leaves for another post elsewhere his departure implies not only a physical separation from the city itself but also the growth of social distance from his circle. 'The person who leaves gets more distant day by day' sums it all up; hence the strong sense of tragedy that the Japanese feel in farewells.

There is no alienation, loneliness or irritability comparable to that of the Japanese whose work takes him to a foreign country. 'They've probably completely forgotten me', and 'That colleague of mine back home has probably played his cards so well that he'll be a manager in no time' – such apprehensions suggest the wretched atmosphere built round himself by the Japanese exile. To diminish the sense of separation a little, he writes letters diligently. But to those he left back in Japan he 'gets more distant day by day', so the replies gradually get fewer and further between, and finally non-business connections cease entirely. He becomes weary of waiting for the order to return home and when at last the long-awaited permission is granted and he returns to his old job it somehow just is not the same. It is clearly a social 'minus' to have been away. He will have to spend an uncomfortable period until he again becomes accustomed and readjusted to his old group, the climate of which may well have changed since he left. In fact, it often happens that the promotion of a man who has stayed abroad for a certain period of time is delayed longer than that of his colleagues (dōryō) who have served continuously in the main office. This does not necessarily apply, of course, in the case of a company where business requires able men to reside abroad; in this case the various branch offices abroad are ranked on the regular promotion ladder. Even so, however, the man posted abroad finds it hard not to feel out of the mainstream of developments in his firm's affairs. Most Japanese men abroad are quite homesick, and very concerned with personnel affairs in the home office. It is not surprising, then, that the Japanese does not like to leave his own community for very long periods; he is very prone to the apprehension that too long a period of absence will lead automatically to an inability to keep up-to-date and to retain standards. This means being excluded from the activities of his old group.

In contrast with the Japanese ideal of group participation, a group formed on the basis of attribute maintains ties with a member no matter where he lives or works, because of its network, which can overcome separation in terms of both space and time. Thus an Indian or Chinese living abroad can get on with his work calmly and live comfortably because of the existence of this network. Further, an Indian born in Africa or elsewhere abroad could go back to live in his grandfather's village and his presence would be taken for granted. He would be received easily by the villagers, even though they did not know his face, or even his father's or grandfather's. They would accept him because he is linked to the village by patrilineal kinship.

But a Japanese in similar circumstances would have to face a very uncomfortable situation and would not be likely to summon the courage to go back to live in his grandfather's village. The villagers would say, 'That is a new face that we don't know'; they would say to him, 'Nobody remembers your grandfather; people of his generation are all dead. Things have changed a lot here.' He would be treated as an outsider and, even if he were finally accepted, he would probably be placed at the bottom of the hierarchy, without being given the full rights of village membership. He would be expected to make a handsome donation to the communal fund, in the same way as would be expected of any unrelated newcomer. In daily life he would be left alone and would remain outside the social life of the community; because his habits and interests are quite different from those of the villagers, it would be difficult to arrive at any form of mutual understanding. Here, the invisible kinship link is not adequate to establish the legitimacy of the relation between him and the villagers. But in a Hindu community legitimacy of kinship survives against the ruptures of time and space to preserve the personal relation.

A Japanese who has been away from his home village for a long period is reluctant to go back, even though he usually has a sentimental attachment to it. He will say, 'My parents are already dead, my brothers and sisters are very old, it's now the turn of my nephews. You can't expect anything from them.' Or, 'It's a new generation since I went away. I don't know them well.' Kinship linkage may, however, have rather more efficacy in the reverse case, when a cousin, nephew or niece from the home village asks for the help of the ex-villager on moving to the city where the latter lives.

Ties of kinship, friendship or group membership all tend to diminish through physical separation. Even a reduction in the frequency of meetings with a friend causes one's rights and voice in the relationship to decrease accordingly. It has long been true that a Japanese who knows the Chinese and the English well has been deeply impressed by and has even envied the constancy and steadiness of their personal relationships in spite of long periods of separation. Tangibility in a personal relationship is a vital element in the creation of unity, particularly in a group which has no universal rules, but there is little equipment to resist breaches made by time and space. Even for a person physically present in the group, an emotional clash could entail the loss of a friendship. Tangibility is a very unstable support for the group. But at the same time it does facilitate the achievement of a condition in which recruitment is always open at the bottom of the hierarchy and in which anyone can be a candidate. Though it contributes to instability, it also offers the opportunity to adjust in the face of changing circumstances.

To summarize: while a Japanese attaches great importance to concreteness and appreciates readiness to react to a changing situation, he does not trust nor establish a universal law, the nature of which is to be divorced from immediate actuality, although adaptable to any circumstance. Japan has no native concept of 'organization' or 'network' abstracted or divorced from actual man; 'organization' is perceived as a kind of succession of direct and concrete relationships between man and man. Man's concrete existence itself forms a part of 'organization'. This is to be seen very clearly, for example, in the development of residential areas in the suburbs of a large city. Private houses are built sporadically, in-filling follows and when, in the course of time, there grow clusters of houses residents realize the need for roads and, finally, narrow roads will be built, winding in such a way as to serve every house in the cluster. Such irregularity is not confined to the roads but is to be found also in the numbering of the houses, which goes by the order in which they were built rather than by the geographical order of the blocks or the location of the house unit. As a result, house numbering is in no way logical, and the stranger cannot possibly find a house simply by its number.

It is indeed surprising that little effort is made – by either planners or residents – to build roads or lay down plans for blocks or areas before work begins on the houses. The vast residential areas of Tokyo are the most telling example of the Japanese concept of 'organization'; these areas spread, literally, like amoeba! Surprisingly enough, processes such as these have improved hardly at all during the last hundred years, in contrast with the startling developments in industry. Certainly one can find the occasional well-planned residential area built by one of the large estate companies, but this is the exception; the more regular circumstances indicate the strength of the indigenous social forces in the face of great technical improvements. Techniques can easily be imported and improved, but it is very difficult to change the inherent system of social organization.

Tangibility, the essential element in 'organization' for the Japanese, may well have some bearing also on Japanese religious concepts. Japanese culture has no conception of a God existing abstractly, completely separate from the human world. In the ultimate analysis, the Japanese consciousness of the object of religious devotion grows out of direct-contact relations between individuals; it is conceived as an extension of this mediating tie. What is termed ancestor worship in Japan is quite different from that of the Chinese: it visualizes and is based on a concrete conception of ancestors in a series of generations going back directly from the dead parent to the founder of the house in which the family is domiciled. The recognized lineage of ancestors is fairly short, hardly going back further than those forefathers who live in the memory as quite concrete personal figures. Even the Emperor, with his ancestors, is conceptualized as the ultimate figure of successive lineal extensions of such actual links common to all Japanese through their respective ancestors: he is not a sacred figure divorced from his people.

Concluding Remarks

The analysis presented in the previous chapters of various Japanese group organizations reveals the vertical structural principle, the core of which is to be found in the basic social relationship between two individuals. This structural tendency, developing in the course of the history of the Japanese people, has become one of the characteristics of Japanese culture.

Certain factors have encouraged this tendency. The first is the homogeneous configuration of Japanese society. Archaeological research has shown that during the Jōmon period a single culture spread over the whole of Japan: between this time and the beginning of the historical period (fifth century A D), continental culture along with wet paddy cultivation may have left a considerable influence, particularly in western Japan, and may have helped the development of the Japanese state formation, but the number of continentals actually moving into Japan seems to have been very small, and these were quickly and readily absorbed into the native population, so that there is no indication that these new elements formed a separate stratum from the Japanese. There is no evidence of significant movement into the islands of non-Japanese after this period.

Local powers and cultures developed during the medieval period, but these were no more than variations of the native pattern. During the Tokugawa period the centralized feudal system under the Shogunate assisted the development of an institutional homogeneity on top of the basic cultural homogeneity. In Tokugawa Japan peasants formed more than 80 per cent of the population, the *samurai* – the top status group – accounted for a further 6 per cent and the remainder consisted of merchants, craftsmen, priests and unregistered minor groups. The classification of *samurai* included nearly two hundred feudal lords and their retainers together with the retainers of the Tokugawa Shogunate. They were like modern bureaucrats, in that they lived on a salary, which was paid in rice and differentiated by status, and were sharply separated from the peasants. Unlike the upper strata of pre-modern England, Europe, India and China, they were neither landed aristocracy nor merchants.

Social stratification in terms of *samurai* and peasants was based on Tokugawa policy and backed by the law; it was not that social differentiation was a product of economic development. In addition, the *samurai* group was so insignificant in number that this kind of stratification has no sociological significance in the matter of the total configuration. It would be more correct to regard the *samurai* as a kind of bureaucrat, although his status was hereditary. It is for this reason that the line between *samurai* and peasant became blurred so rapidly after 'modernization' and the effective development of a modern educational and bureaucratic system. As administrators or intellectuals under the centralized system, the *samurai* contributed to the spread of a uniform national culture.

Peasant communities were very homogeneous and peasants were separated locally from other occupational groups. Although there were, of course, poor and wealthy, the differences were relative and not significant (the majority were smallholders), so that no distinct status group, such as gentry and poor landless peasants, ever developed within a community. There grew, on the contrary, a strong sense of solidarity within each distinct village community; though there were relative rankings of upper and lower or of rich and poor within a community, these differences did not create constant status groups cutting across different villages. This means, in effect, that the majority of the Japanese people have not been historically conditioned to life in a stratified communuity with effective lines of demarcation between groups. They are accustomed to regard ranking rather than stratification as an organizational principle.

A man living in a society with this organizational basis and cultural background believes in basic equality and communal rights; while he is conscious of delicately graded rankings among his fellows, he will not recognize overt stratification in his world. Such a mentality appears in all manner of group activities. As an appropriate illustration, it is applicable to the Japanese concept of 'democracy'. Indeed, if the outsider is to understand this concept he must be aware of this mentality.

'Democracy' as a symbolic term grew roots in Japan immediately after the second world war, along with an appreciation of a set of cultural elements from America. Its usage, so fashionable in Japan and other parts of Asia, does not have the same connotation as in the West; in Japan, for example, it relates not to a form of government but to a form of relationship. This usage seems strange to the West. For example:

> At the same time, one has to take care that one does not misinterpret what the Japanese mean by 'democracy', a word they constantly use. It does not mean social equality; the consideration, for example, shown one's equals and official superiors is not extended to those below. 'Democracy' does seem to mean a way of doing business that combines commitment and high principle with lack of factionalism and internecine conflict. People refer to organizations as 'undemocratic' if there is no harmony or consensus. Thus, democracy and politics would seem antithetical. (David Riesman, *Conversations in Japan*, New York, 1967, p. 202.)

The reason why 'democracy' became so fashionable after the war seems to be that the Japanese found it a useful term for demeaning the old 'feudal' or 'authoritarian' pattern of the Japanese social and political systems. 'Democracy' represents a negative reaction against the operation of the pre-war system, which gave authority to a higher sector in an organization. In the Japanese system a higher position in a hierarchical organization could hold unlimited power or privilege against the lower, since there is no clear-cut delineation of assigned rôles between higher and lower.

It is in this sociological and psychological soil that the imported term 'democracy' has developed its specific Japanese connotation. It is used particularly as a charge against the monopoly of power by a privileged sector or a stronger faction in an organization. It is interesting to observe, however, that the form in which this charge is stated is identical with that through which authoritarian power has been exercised. The change from 'feudalism' to 'democracy' is not structural or organizational; it is rather a change in the direction of the motion of energy within the same pipeline, this energy exerted by the same kinds of people.

What the Japanese mean by 'democracy' is a system that should take the side of, or give consideration to, the weaker or lower; in practice, any decision should be made on the basis of a consensus which includes those located lower in the hierarchy. Such a consensus – reached by what might be termed maximum consultation – might seem a by-product of the post-war 'democratic' age; yet it is not at all new to the Japanese, representing as it does a very basic style of the traditional group operation. The exercise of power or unilateral decision-making on the part of the top sector of a group co-existed with unanimous decision-making on the basis of maximum consultation. The difference between these two procedures, as I see it, derives from differences in the internal composition of a group (such as scale or manner) not in kinds of groups – such as differences in occupation, between rural and urban or younger and older.

The small group, of a dozen or less, with no significant status or economic differentiation between members, is most likely to function 'democratically' in the Japanese sense. Good examples of such a group can be found among many old-established villages, where the tradition has been to base any decision on maximum consultation. In addition to regular meetings, emergency gatherings are held whenever an urgent or major issue faces the village. To such a meeting every household sends a representative, normally the household head; in his absence, his wife or grown son deputizes. Such a meeting consists, ideally, of about ten persons. A village is always organized by subgroups (local corporate groups) consisting of about ten households, and it is in these important functional groups that primary meetings are frequently held.

This is the size of gathering which the Japanese find most satisfactory and enjoyable. It is usual in such a gathering for every participant, whether he be poor and lower in rank or not, to express an opinion. Relaxed and informal talk at the start induces a free atmosphere, as a kind of warm-up for the meeting proper. It is most important that a meeting should reach a unanimous conclusion; it should leave no one frustrated or dissatisfied, for this weakens village or group unity and solidarity. The undercurrent of feeling is: 'After all we are in the same boat, and we should live peacefully without leaving anyone behind.' It does not matter how much time and trouble are required to reach unanimity; what matters is that all should play their part in reaching a final consensus.

The process of discussion is not necessarily logical. They will talk about this and that, often with much indulgence towards any individual feelings at stake. A meeting may be adjourned if a deadlock is reached, and will be resumed later in a fresh mood. In the course of time dissension decreases, and consent increases. When a point is reached where support comes from about seventy per cent of the members, this is the sign that consensus is near. In the final stage the minority makes a concession, saying, 'I will join, since all of you have agreed. Though I dissent in this particular issue, I am very ready to co-operate with you, and at any rate I have been able to say all that I wanted to say'.

However, the procedure of a meeting of a large group does not allow sufficient time and, of course, the degree of differentiation in status and interest is much greater: as a result, members know less of each other, and many of them are reluctant to speak out. Such factors help to make the procedure of decision-making in these circumstances 'undemocratic'; the process is influenced by top members or a dominant clique and governed by the principle of majority rule, with scope for the effective use of hierarchical power relationships.

The urge towards maximum consultation, regardless of the nature and size of a group, frequently results in interminably long meetings, dragged out in the name of 'democracy'. Japan is today the land of meetings, and it is far from difficult to find a man who spends more time at meetings than at his desk. In group operation on the Japanese system there are few established rules and rôles are not clearly defined or distinguished, so that not only vital issues but those less pertinent are brought under consideration by a meeting. 'Democratic' procedure does not, of course, contribute to efficient modern management; but those at the top can make it a convenient excuse for a show of 'democracy', while, in fact, the decision is made by a 'boss' or influential members of the group, in disregard even of the function of the chairman. 'Democracy' may be in popular demand, but the old hierarchical structure functions latently under the façade and format of 'democracy'.

Apart from what he calls the 'democratic' procedure, how does the Japanese man see his organization? A Japanese cannot tolerate open discrimination by groups or strata. To illustrate this kind of feeling, there is the story of a *sarariman* who was approached by one of the western firms in Japan, looking for well-qualified Japanese staff. He was quite interested in the offer, which was far better than his job in a Japanese firm. However, he declined the offer because he had been told by a friend employed in a western firm that only executives (westerners) took coffee-breaks, while the Japanese subordinate staff stayed at work. This prompted in him a sense of discrimination and humiliation. Although in Japanese firms top executives are often absent from their desks to attend weddings and funeral ceremonies or to play golf, these are readily accepted by subordinates as the social duties of the man at the top, who would sometimes share coffee or a drink with his staff. But it is difficult for a Japanese to accept that those at the top of an organization should take a coffee-break while their subordinates remain at work.

The privileges of those at the top in Japanese groups can be seen in various ways, perhaps more obviously in their behaviour towards subordinates. The Japanese can tolerate a vertical, one-to-one power relationship between two people directly linked to each other, but this is not accepted in the form of a class or group. Here we see a direct link with the experience of peasants in earlier times. There is no obvious status group formed by masters or landlords, excluding peasants: on the contrary, a functional group was formed by landlord and tenant, master and servant, and the master or superior was always one of them in the same group. The personal relationship in Japan between superior and subordinate may give an impression of wide disparity on formal occasions – a subordinate usually being a 'yes-man', with much bowing to his superior; but this is counter-balanced by informal contacts which give the subordinate a feeling of being a member of the same household. The Japanese boss, consciously or unconsciously, displays to his subordinates on occasions a kind of behaviour in which the power relation of the formal organization is reversed, with the theory that, when all are in the same boat, everyone should enjoy communal rights, regardless of difference in status and contribution. There is strong opposition to the formation of status groups within a single community, although the order of higher and lower in relationships between individuals is readily accepted.

It seems from these and similar considerations that Japanese 'democracy' is a kind of community sentiment, with, as a major premise, a high degree of cohesion and consensus within the group. Liberalism with respect to opinion is not part of the concept, for 'democracy' may well be interpreted in terms of freedom of speech, by which is meant the freedom of the lower or the underprivileged to speak out; there is, however neither wish for opposition nor realization of the function of opposition. In Japan it is extremely difficult to engage in a truly democratic discussion (of the type that I know from experience is common in India or, for instance, in Italy, England or America), in the course of which the statements of opposition are taken by the other party and then form an important element in the development of the discussion.

The Japanese interpretation of 'democracy', added to the characteristics and the value orientation already discussed, contributes to the strengthening of the solidarity of a group built of members of different qualification and status. The egalitarianism in the workings of a group, as has been noticed earlier (see p. 38), stands in the way of the formulation and the development of the concept of specialization and the incorporation of similar groups. We might well here recall the earlier discussion, in which was proposed the theory that the absence of division of labour assisted the development of the vertical system. Also important in this analysis is the absence of any type of organizational principle based on kinship networks as well as any sharp distinction between kin and non-kin. Since kinship factors cannot be used as an effective and primary charter of group organization, the bases are the locality and constant and tangible personal relations. I have already presented an analysis of the traditional rural community;* we now find the same principle in operation in modern communities.

The changes in Japanese society in the course of modernization have attracted much research and discussion. It has often been argued that war brought a fundamental change in the Japanese; it might be truer to argue that since the circumstances and supports of life in Japan have altered radically, ideas and attitudes to life have in turn changed, just as clothes are changed with the coming spring after the cold winter. It is Japanese nature to accept change with little resistance and, indeed, to welcome and value change; but a superficial change of outlook, as facile as changes in fashion, has not the slightest effect on the firm persistence of the basic nature and core of personal relations and group dynamics.

Historians, sociologists, economists and social critics are concerned to follow processes of change. These may find fault with the analysis presented here as may well those cultural anthropologists who are not accustomed to structural analysis, on the charge that I disregard the changing aspects of Japanese society. In answer I should restate the aim of this study – not to describe Japanese society but to view Japanese social structure in the light of a cross-cultural comparison of social structures; this is the concern of social anthropology which distinguishes it from the other social sciences. I do not for a moment deny the

* See Nakane, *op. cit.*

changing aspects of Japanese society; but I believe that it is also most important to look for the persistent factors underlying the various changes. In a scientific cross-cultural comparison the constants are dealt with more effectively; aspects of change are more attractive for the description of the picture of Japan alone.

It is in informal systems rather than in overt cultural elements that persistent factors are to be found. The informal system, the driving force of Japanese activities, is a native Japanese brew, steeped in a unique characteristic of Japanese culture. In the course of modernization Japan imported many western cultural elements, but these were and are always partial and segmentary and are never in the form of an operating system. It is like a language with its basic indigenous structure or grammar which has accumulated a heavy overlay of borrowed vocabulary; while the oulook of Japanese society has suffered drastic changes over the past hundred years, the basic social grammar has hardly been affected. Here is an example of industrialization and the importation of western culture not effecting changes in the basic cultural structure.

This structural persistence manifests one of the distinctive characteristics of a homogeneous society built on a vertical organizational principle. Such a society is fairly stable; it is difficult to create revolution or disorder on a national scale, since there is segmentation of the lower sectors into various group clusters fenced off from each other. Structural difficulties stand in the way of a broad scope of joint activity – members of a trade union, for example, are too loyal to their own company to join forces with their brothers in other company unions; student unions are unable to muster the great majority of students, but develop groups where the solidarity of one group differentiates it from another. A union movement, a confrontation, whether between manager and workers or between faculty and students, is always carried on within an institution, although it causes echoes generally and politically. It is like an outbreak of domestic discord, and so tends to be very emotional and radical. In an extreme case it may even drive some directors and section heads to suicide. At the height of the student revolt, three directors committed suicide, and there were similar instances during union movements in the industrial sector in the very early post-war period. These movements arouse intense sympathies or reactions on the part of all concerned, but this is in stark contrast with the peaceful order of the social life of the general public which surrounds them. Thus trade or student unions and other popular movements, in spite of the strong appeal of radicalism and violence, have little social significance, in that they are unable to stir the majority, even of those in the same category.

Thus there is a cruelly heavy handicap against the powerless and the socially inferior. Indeed, there is no possibility of creating any kind of revolution. A rebellion against the bosses and appeals to the general public may result in some changes in public opinion, but will never succeed in changing the social structure. At the same time, although those at the top can as a group exercise power and influence to check these movements, an individual, however able, however strong his personality and high his status, has to compromise with his group's decision, which then develops a life of its own. Once a collective decision of this kind has been formulated, no individual can check or turn it, and he must simply wait for the time when the tide turns by itself; he is like a farmer cultivating wet paddy who must await the good weather that follows a typhoon.

However, it is the inherent mental make-up of the Japanese that allows the formulation of such over-riding group decisions. One of the factors dominating Japanese thinking and aspiration is *relativism*, the constant desire to rise a little higher than the average; to put it in a Japanese way, 'a desire to be on a level similar to the other person who is supposed to be higher than oneself'. The Japanese have no religious practice or belief that controls individual thinking and behaviour on the strength of a supernatural being; the vital rôle is played not by religion or philosophy but by a very human morality. The yardstick of this morality is always determined by contemporary trends. The feeling that 'I must do this because A and B also do it' or 'they will laugh at me unless I do such-and-such' rules the life of the individual with greater force than any other consideration and thus has a deep effect on decision-making. Agreed, there are those who maintain a 'going my way' attitude, but these are exceptionally rare in Japanese society. It has been noted that the younger generation is becoming more critical of this general attitude, and this tendency may well weaken its force in the course of time. Nevertheless, for the moment, this deeply rooted social habit still continues as a dominant tendency. It is partly because they are based on such attitudes that the ideals of the Japanese are more liable to veer with the shift of the times than those of other societies. And it is from this source that there derives the 'lack of consistency' or the 'high degree of adaptability' that so often forms part of the description of the Japanese character.

Majority rule is a powerful device in the hands of a dominant group or sector of a group; the power at the top, always a dominant group and never an individual, always succeeds in imposing its aims, with even the law powerless to offer any check. It is obvious that political rather than social traits are decisive in such a society, and throughout Japan's history political activities have been more important than any other. This is the clue to Japan's efficiency – but it is also a source of danger, to Japanese society as a whole and to the groups which constitute it.

Index

Index

Index

Index

More about Penguins
and Pelicans

Penguinews, which appears every month, contains details
of all the new books issued by Penguins as they are
published. From time to time it is supplemented by
Penguins in Print, which is a complete list of all available
books published by Penguins. (There are well over four
thousand of these.)

A specimen copy of *Penguinews* will be sent to you free
on request. For a year's issues (including the complete
lists) please send 30p if you live in the United Kingdom,
or 60p if you live elsewhere. Just write to Dept EP,
Penguin Books Ltd, Harmondsworth, Middlesex,
enclosing a cheque or postal order, and your name will be
added to the mailing list.

Note: *Penguinews* and *Penguins in Print* are not
available in the U.S.A. or Canada

Japanese Imperialism Today

Jon Halliday and Gavan McCormack

The empire of the yen is now third only to those of the dollar and the rouble. Nevertheless there is a surprising dearth of detailed information in the West about Japanese trade and industry.

In what is avowedly a Marxist study of Asian economics the authors of this Pelican limit themselves to documenting, tabulating and (to some extent) analysing Japan's economic and political relations in the area of South-East Asia, scrutinizing these within the context of her special ties with the United States. This is the area which has provided a springboard for the legendary post-war success of a country which lacks almost all major raw materials.

Since, clearly, their subject cannot be handled in isolation, the authors devote a chapter to Japan's relations with China and two appendices to her dealings with the Soviet Union and Australasia. And in one crucial chapter they reveal the speed and extent of Japan's rearmament – to a point where she can 'turn nuclear' very rapidly.

A History of Modern Japan

Richard Storry

The rise, fall, and renaissance of Japan, within the space
of less than a hundred years, is one of the most curious
and dramatic stories of our time. This history begins by
describing the historical background to Japan's emergence
as a modern state in the sixties of the last century. It then
discusses in detail the stages of Japan's advance as a
world power up to the tragedy of the Pacific War. This
struggle and its aftermath – the Occupation – are vividly
described and analysed. The last chapter, bringing the
account right up to the present day, is a fascinating study
of the new Japan that has come into being since the San
Francisco Peace Treaty of 1951.

'There has long been a need for an up-to-date general
survey of Japanese history. This book . . . admirably fills
the gap . . . Mr Storry has provided a succinct, well-written,
and accurate account' – *International Affairs*